THE HIDDEN SELF GROWN STRONG IN GOD
THE COLLECTED ESSAYS OF
FATHER GEORGE ASCHENBRENNER, S.J.

GEORGE A. ASCHENBRENNER, S.J.

En Route Books and Media, LLC
Saint Louis, MO

⚓ENROUTE
Make the time

En Route Books and Media, LLC
5705 Rhodes Avenue
St. Louis, MO 63109

Contact us at contactus@enroutebooksandmedia.com

ISBN-13: 979-8-88870-411-0
Library of Congress Control Number: Available online at
https://catalog.loc.gov

Cover design by Timothy D. Boatright of Vistra Communications in Tampa, Florida using Saint Ignatius of Loyola by Peter Paul Rubens (circa 1620)

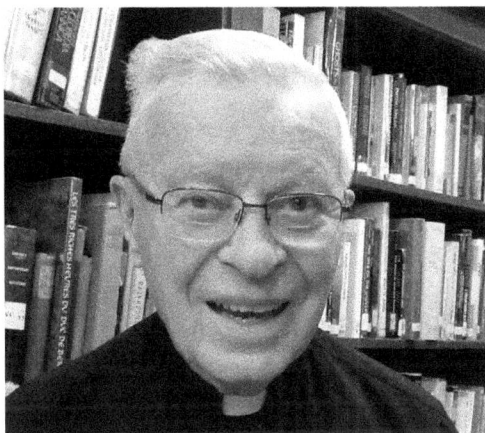

Father George Aschenbrenner, S.J., (1932-2021) was raised in Reading, Pennsylvania and graduated from St. Joseph's College in Philadelphia with a degree in English. He entered the Society of Jesus in 1954 and received both his Licentiate in Philoso- phy and Sacred Theology before being ordained to the priest- hood in 1965. In addition to serving six years as the Director of Spiritual Formation at the North American College in Rome, Father Aschenbrenner was the Novice Master at the Jesuit Novitiate of St. Isaac Jogues in Wernersville, Pennsylva- nia and later became Director of the Jesuit Center for Spiri- tual Growth. He has also served as a retreat director at the University of Scranton and St. Joseph's University. In 1994, he became one of the founders of The Institute for Priestly Formation where he lectured regularly on diocesan priestly spirituality and identity and also directed seminarians and priests in the Spiritual Exercises of St. Ignatius Loyola. He is the author of *Quickening the Fire in Our Midst: The Challenge of Diocesan Priestly Spirituality* and *Stretched for Greater Glory: What to Expect from the Spiritual Exercises.*

TABLE OF CONTENTS

FOREWORD

The interior formation of priests is a vital ministry for the holiness and the pastoral health of the Church. Few spiritual guides have better contributed to this formation than Father George Aschenbrenner, S.J. Over his decades of ordained ministry, Father Aschenbrenner has assisted countless priests and their formators in grasping the essential role that prayer and discernment play in their own well-being and in the fruitfulness of their ministerial endeavors. In this book, you will find the best of Father Aschenbrenner's written contributions to the spiritual life of priests. I encourage both priests and seminary formators to read and study these pages and to reap the benefits of his wisdom and experience as a pivotal spiritual director for our age.

I first met Father Aschenbrenner when I was a sophomore in high school and he was a newly ordained priest. He was helping to conduct a summer session for Sodality leaders in Jesuit high schools on prayer and meditation and the public prayer of the Liturgy. I have been pleased to hear him speak many times since then. I am particularly pleased to see the essays: "Monasticism of the Heart" and "Abandonment That Enlivens and Sets Fire for Mission" in the pages that follow. These essays are very important for the person and ministry of priests, but they also bear on essential truths that are important for the life of the Church today. Additionally, the essays are written beautifully and in the best sense "edify" or build up the faith, the Church, and the priesthood in our time. There is substance in these matters, not just a liquid vagueness.

I commend the accumulated wisdom of these pages to all clergy, and I thank Father Aschenbrenner for his many years of priestly service—a genuine treasury of good. He is a gift to the Church, to priestly formation, and to all who benefit from the charism of St. Ignatius of Loyola's "Spiritual Exercises."

Cardinal Daniel DiNardo
Archbishop of Galveston-Houston

INTRODUCTION

Several decades ago, Father George Aschenbrenner, S.J., emerged as a leader in the search to recapture the original spirit and practice of the Spiritual Exercises of St. Ignatius Loyola. His groundbreaking writing on the "Consciousness Examen" breathed new life into the practice of the daily Examen Prayer, which had always been a vital component in the formation and life of religious women and men. His early mission as a Jesuit focused mainly on guiding the candidates of the Maryland Province of the Society of Jesus as their novice master. In addition, he served many communities of women religious who benefited from his talks and retreats.

Providentially, a Jesuit provincial suggested that Father Aschenbrenner begin to turn his attention to work also with diocesan priests. This new focus found him journeying to Rome where he served for a term as Director of Spiritual Formation at the Pontifical North American College, the formation house for United States seminarians studying in Rome. Even after completing his time in Rome, he continued to offer retreats and conferences to priests in many dioceses.

In 1981, while speaking at a meeting of diocesan seminary spiritual directors, Father Aschenbrenner spontaneously put together some suggestions for a spiritual formation

1

program that he hoped would impact the hearts and lives of diocesan seminarians. While carefully preserving the unique characteristics of diocesan priestly life and spirituality, as distinguished from that of monastic or religious priests, he called for a "kind of novitiate for diocesan seminarians."

About ten years later, those suggestions would be developed and realized in what became The Institute for Priestly Formation (IPF). Father Aschenbrenner's proposals came to particular fruition in IPF's summer program of spiritual formation for diocesan seminarians. As that program began in 1995, Father Aschenbrenner developed his 1981 proposals into a course that he taught for many years in the summer seminarian program. The course eventually blossomed into a book published some years later entitled, *Quickening the Fire in Our Midst: The Challenge of Diocesan Priestly Spirituality*.

With this present publication, The Institute for Priestly Formation wishes to make known to a wider audience a selection of some of Father Aschenbrenner's many articles. In so doing, we also wish to honor him as one of the founders of The Institute for Priestly Formation, located at Creighton University in Omaha, Nebraska. With this book, we hope to voice the gratitude of countless diocesan priests throughout the world who have benefited from Father Aschenbrenner's teaching, his spiritual direction, and his encouragement. May these articles help many priests to serve the Greater Glory of God!

Father Richard Gabuzda
Executive Director, The Institute for Priestly Formation

Section I

Interiority and Prayer

BECOMING WHOM WE CONTEMPLATE

Contemplation is a radically transforming process.
For this reason, many people become fearful of serious
contemplation and either avoid it altogether or practice it
only halfheartedly. As the contemplative process develops,
its challenge and cost become more threatening. But at
the same time, a taste of its joy and intimacy exercises an
alluring attractiveness.

The whole method of Ignatian prayer in the Exercises is
actually a process of interpersonal transformation in faith.
In this interpersonal process, God is carefully and insistently
calling us away from our false self exposing a new self, glorious in this world and ever so much more in eternity. The
process involved in Ignatian contemplation, which is one part
of the Ignatian method of prayer, is also aimed at a deepening interpersonal encounter. This contemplative process also
creates an enlightening, discerning presence in the midst of
the quandaries, opportunities, and choices of our personal
and social daily life.

Because Ignatian prayer gradually peers deeper and
deeper into the heart of mystery, its fruits are never easily
described. The most profound realities of life are usually so
simple that they leave us at a loss for words. For example, we

stutter and stammer or revert to "wooden" unhelpful words in describing our experience of a beloved friend. And though friends are always able to find a beautiful full connotation in words, someone outside the experience may either misinterpret the apparent use of a cliché or criticize what seems to them a disproportionate, exaggerated use of language. And so it is with attempting to describe contemplation, mystery, and faith. For this reason, I must presume that the reader's own experience of contemplation and mystery can enrich my simple, struggling statement and, thereby, prevent much misunderstanding. I write here of an experience in faith—but not one that, *within* faith, is not far-fetched or terribly rare. And yet, contemplation is an experience known finally only *in* experience. So I am writing for people who have tasted, in however diluted a fashion, the sweetness of contemplation and because they have tasted it, hunger for it more and more.

Beyond the difficulty of expression and understanding, real danger attends the practice of contemplation. Its cost is steep and serious—nothing less than the death of a very real, but false self. Any complacent contemplation that would struggle to avoid this mortifying conversion, however understandable it may be, is actually a contradiction. Genuine contemplation is always a dangerous encounter with God whose jealousy for our love and our very person surpasses, finally, our stubborn selfishness. Therefore, something much more than a craving for emotional highs and dramatic insights is needed to fuel our practice of contemplation. Only the experienced attractiveness of God's love can encourage our sense of inadequacy and inspire a persevering practice of contemplation.

Ignatian Method in Prayer

Ignatian prayer is easily misunderstood. The multiplicity of details, directives, techniques, and methods presented in the Spiritual Exercises frequently distracts a person from the fundamental dynamic and orientation actually intended. To take care to darken the room, to take care not to bring up pleasing thoughts, to strive to grieve—all of this can seem like a straitjacket of rigid control of environment, mind, and feelings—facilitating frustration and tension rather than simple prayer. Such misunderstanding always betrays a lack of genuine experience of the Exercises.

Rather than being a repressive restriction of spontaneity and freedom, Ignatian method in prayer is really a matter of progressive concentration and integrative assimilation of a human person's powers in an interpersonal encounter of love. The movement from "Contemplation" to "Repetition" to "Application of Senses" is truly a method, a method carefully paced and attuned to a heart's profound desire for simplicity and intimacy in a shared commitment. It is the method or process of a human person's entering ever more thoroughly into the mysterious union of love. Only truths and beauties that get to the heart, the emotions, and the sensibilities can deeply affect a person and make that person really care, thus, making love ready for the details of daily living.[1]

This method and development in prayer reveals Ignatius' genuine sense of human development and his great concern for the thorough, dependable commitment of human love. We cannot settle for mere reasonable weighing of the things of God in consideration, nor for the thinking and daydreaming about God in meditation. But all this invites us further in contemplation to let God, in Jesus, happen to us and transform our whole affective presence in the world. We will need to be with God again and again in repetition if our commitment in love is to become sensually alive and responsibly effective through the application of our senses and all the psycho-sexual energies of our identity. Ignatian method in prayer, then, facilitates a person's development in the intimate assimilation of faith with God whose love, as revealed in Jesus, quickens us to loving service now and to a longing for fullness in eternity. In the Ignatian method of prayer, as in all contemplation—and in any genuine love, too—we become whom we contemplate.

Divine Initiative and Mortification

Although Ignatian prayer's transforming assimilation of us into the Jesus of God always requires much patient, regular work on our part, from the beginning to the end, all the effort and activity springs from love—God's love for each one of us. Rather than something Pelagian, something performed on our own, the hard work of contemplation is always anteceded by our loving God's boundless desire for each one of us and is inspired by our touch, feel, and taste for such a fact in faith. The art of sensitivity to Divine desire and love always takes precedence over, but does not excuse one from, the science of human techniques of prayer. The initiative, whether we consciously realize it or not, is with God whose beautifully loving ways are always wooing our hearts. And so, all the regular, patient effort at prayer on our part is response, never our own initiative—always a response in careful cooperation with God whose love and desire for us will always far exceed our struggling effort.

Without a proper sense of the Divine initiative in contemplation, the cost and sacrifice of the venture either becomes too much or is dealt with in a very unhealthy manner. Serious contemplation is always a mortifying experience. For a new self to be born, for each of us to become the one whom we contemplate, an insidiously false self must die. Without an attractive intimation of all that we can become in Jesus, the prospective death of our very real self-centeredness can overwhelm and petrify us. Or deficient experience of God's inspiring love can instigate an onslaught against self-centeredness that will undercut healthy self-acceptance—the necessary foundation for all human, spiritual development.

Without the mortification of our deceitful self, the process of Ignatian prayer cannot achieve its goal: the revelation in all its beauty of a new self in Jesus. This mortification and revelation, this dying and rising, is a process and tension within which we live our daily lives. On this earth, one is never had without the other. We all know those exhilarating moments when the integration of these two aspects, rather than making us tense, stretches and thrills us to the intensity of enthusiastic love. But we also slip and slide and lose this decisive integrity of our inner life whenever we mistakenly try to find life and truth in our false self. The daily asceticism of going against (*agere contra*) our false and desolate self gives birth and decisive clarity to a new self revealed in our contemplation of God's love in Jesus. This asceticism, an essential component of any mysticism, has often in the past been misunderstood in too "un-nuanced" a way as a simple "going against self." Without the careful qualification of which self we are going against, which self we are to die to, our practice of the spiritual life can become either unhealthy or shoddy and plagued with overreaction to a past misunderstanding. Much of the aimlessness, gloom, and anger of the 1960's and 1970's may have resulted from such confusions of the spiritual life. At times, an unhealthy loss of self-acceptance and self-confidence results from a destructive "going against" the self. On the other hand, an understandably angry reaction to or a hazy disregard for advice simply to go against self produces in many an unascetical sloppiness that prevents much decisive inner intensity and clarity.

In all this concern for a mortifying asceticism, the Divine initiative must never be forgotten. Otherwise, the mystical goal of Ignatian prayer will be overlooked—and with disastrous consequences. Ignatius was accused of preferring ascetics to mystics. This misunderstanding fails to realize that the power to go against our false self is a mystical grace born of and fired by desire for God's transforming and satisfying love.[2] Because of Ignatius's fierce desire that God's love transform our human hearts and world, his method in prayer— always geared toward an interpersonal experience of God's unifying love—acknowledges the necessary interrelationship of contemplation and mortification. He claimed that a mortified person "would easily accomplish more prayer in a quarter of an hour than another who is not mortified would do in two hours."[3] Ignatius saw very clearly that his great concern for "finding God in all things" would always be in direct proportion to his "being mortified in all things." And this mortification, as mentioned above, is really an experience of God, not a repressive denial of self. It is such an experience of God's love that it can expand and enthuse a human heart with that joyous intensity for which our hearts are always yearning and struggling. In this way, the process of Ignatian prayer can bring us to what is everyone's most coveted revelation: a new self, discovered as we enter and share the lively intimacy of Jesus with the one he called "my dear Father." "Christ plays in ten thousand places, lovely in limbs and lovely in eyes not his, to the Father, through the features of men's faces."[4]

A Trinitarian Experience

From the Second Week on, Ignatian contemplation plays a major role in the Exercises, and this contemplation is an explicitly Trinitarian experience. The contemplation on the Incarnation focuses on nothing less than the Trinity itself as the continuing object of all further contemplation in the Exercises. Though the prayer style can seem simple, with a certain child-like quality, the "matter" being contemplated is awesome: a creator God revealing in the precious human details of Jesus a Spirit of such intimate love and faithful forgiveness as to magnetize us for a whole new life. The material in the scenes of the life of Jesus can, at times, seem so ordinary and pedestrian that we misunderstand the loftiness of the venture. Or a self-conscious fear of lofty Trinitarian nature and of these contemplations can rob us of our courage and plague us with a doubting lack of confidence. For this reason, in the Second Week, retreatants often need to renew an act of trust in the Spirit—even more lively within them after the purification of the First Week and now more eager than they realize—to compose them contemplatively with the inner life of God revealed in the beauty of Jesus.

As each contemplation is repeated and passes into another, we are glimpsing more and more clearly the very inner life and heart of God in the tone of voice, gaze of eyes,

touch of hand—all those wonderful human details of Jesus.
Karl Rahner makes the point very forcefully:

> Then the gaze into the face of Jesus of Nazareth is
> changed into the face-to-face vision of God, even if
> both the encounter with Jesus and the consequent vision
> of God only make their presence fully known when the
> confinement of our poor body is split open by death.[5]

As the astonishing reality of what is actually happening to
us in these simple contemplations dawns—and there will
always be a special, privileged moment of realization—we
are halted in the awesome reverence of wonder. A beauty
beyond words! An invitation to let go and become whom we
are contemplating. What an apostolic impulse to serve faith!
What an apostolic impulse to promote justice! A whole new
life beckons us. God, reaching out to save us (and the world)
in Jesus. If we let this process of contemplation have its way
within us, an inner composure of consciousness develops
that will slowly transform our presence to the ordinariness of
daily life. And so, if we oversimplify Ignatian contemplation,
so as to back down from and avoid its genuine Trinitarian
mysticism, we not only make Ignatian prayer superficial but
we also cheapen the quality of our presence and activity in
the world.

The Process of Contemplation

As seen earlier, the whole dynamic of Ignatian prayer
is a progressive movement toward greater interpersonal
involvement with a God in Jesus. Contemplation, as one part
of the whole Ignatian method in prayer, has built right into
its structure a very similar process. From the additions[6] and
the preparatory prayer,[7] right through the closing colloquy,

everything aims at facilitating the careful, loving composition of a whole person with the awesomely renewing mystery of God's love in Jesus.

The additions invite a genuine sense of presence both to God and to ourselves as we stand at the doorway of contemplation. The effort to concentrate our powers, in an acknowledgement of God's loving presence to us here and now, brings an awareness of the thoughts, feelings, moods and desires alive within us at this moment. A lively sense of both God's loving gaze upon us (we are the apple of God's eye[8]) and of God's eagerness to communicate and be with us at this precise time must motivate our effort at concentration.[9] This awareness of God's readiness can open and poise our own hearts in hopeful anticipation of the ensuing encounter. The preparatory prayer actually gives words to this humble openness, this poised eagerness for praise and service of a faithfully loving God—attitudes without which no genuine interpersonal encounter is possible.

In the Second Week, the first prelude is the history. Rather than an objective recalling of the facts of a certain Gospel scene, this week begins to involve us personally with the mystery to be contemplated. Rather than a concern for objective details of past incidents, this week personally involves us here and now with the "how" and "why" of the mystery. For example, in the contemplation on the Incarnation, our concern is not simply with the fact in faith. Ignatius's narration of the history reveals that his chief concern is with the *how* and *why* details that personalize the Trinity's decision, in the face of our human blindness and sinfulness, to "work the redemption of the human race."[10] All the following contemplations in the Exercises spring from and reveal further this paschal decision in the heart of the Trinity. At times, the *how* and *why* of this decision will shine forth from the tone of voice and the look on the face of Jesus of Nazareth in some specific interpersonal encounter of His earthly life. So the first prelude of history does not focus on the past. Rather, it begins personally to involve us with the mystery that is always alive and available here and now: a God, forgiving and saving each and every one of us beyond any merit or power of our own.

The second prelude furthers this ongoing contemplative composition of ourselves with the mystery. Seeing the place is not a whimsical pictorializing of a scene. Our imaginative powers, stirred in faith and treasuring the Gospel details of a particular incident, further engage us, concretely, with all the powers of our person, in the beautiful details of the mystery of our God whose heart in Jesus is always set on saving us. In this way, the encounter begun in the history-prelude is personalized even more by entering into the local conditions of time and place in the mystery. This "entering into" is not a matter of detached objectivity. Nor is it a matter of self-fabricating the details of a scene in a flight of fancy. Rather, the imagination can bring an intimate, a subjective feel for, and a carefully centered concentration on, the details that give local color to the mystery—the mystery ever old and ever new, of the innate attractiveness of God's saving love winning human hearts. As this composition of ourselves with the mystery deepens, we are gradually becoming whom we contemplate.

The third prelude to Ignatian contemplation involves a begging for the grace genuinely desired. Because our hearts can house a great diversity of inner experiences, it is never easy—in the midst of unruly impulses, false expectations, unpredictable moods, selfish needs and flight fancies—to recognize the genuine profound desires of our heart, desires that situate us within centuries of mature humanity. Ignatius was led so deeply into human experience that he puts into words the perennial, true desires formative of the mature human heart. Though finally we can trust Ignatius in his experience and articulation of the true desires of the human heart, usually serious scrutiny and struggle are needed to allow us to discover Ignatius's recommended grace as the genuine and personal desire of our own heart, here and now.

Begging for our heart's true desire can gradually become so persistent that it draws us virtually into identification with that desire. Since these perennial, profound desires are God-given, the process of identification is really a deepening union with God, now known in the yearning of our desire. That this third prelude furthers the interpersonal encounter of Ignatian contemplation becomes even more obvious when we realize that the desire we wanted remains the same all through the Second Week (even in the background of the major Ignatian meditations and considerations of the Two Standards, the Three Types of People, and the Three Ways of Living).

To know Jesus so intimately that intense personal love and enthusiastic following will result is the heart's persistent cry in this part of the Exercises. It is a cry that echoes deep within the realm of mystery, stirs the very heart of God, and brings to our own heart the gradual realization that God is always more involved with us in love than we will ever realize before the surprise of death. Clearly, then, a decisive element in the process of Ignatian contemplation and its transforming union with the beloved is a begging heart's true desire.

As William Peters indicates in his controversial but seminal book on the Exercises, the points in the contemplation of the Second Week are:

> a further development of the preludes, and the contents of the preludes are intensified in the points. . . . "Points" does not primarily refer to a number of consecutive parts of a mystery that is being contemplated but to various activities of the exercitant.[11]

The points involve us in seeing, hearing, inspecting, and considering further what we have already become involved with in the preludes.

> Hence, "points" are only possible once the exercitant has been brought face to face with a reality that is the object of these activities . . . This is the link between preludes and points; the latter are simply impossible without the former.[12]

The points for the contemplation of the Nativity can serve as a model for all other contemplations. The quaint suggestion of imagining ourselves in the cave as a "poor, little, unworthy slave" is simply a way of making ourselves concretely and carefully present in this moment of the one mystery. No looking on from afar will do. Only a presence that will allow contemplating the details of the mystery "with all possible homage and reference"[13] is appropriate to the developing interpersonal experience of One whose love is so set on us that "he might die on the cross, and all this for me."[14]

The process of Ignatian contemplation climaxes in an unrestrained, heart-to-heart colloquy, like the sharing of friends whose intimacy and trust is such that they have nothing to hide or fear. The colloquy is always a development of the grace begged for. But it is a mysterious, unpredictable development—the result of grace inspiring a human mind's logical development of a propositional truth. For this reason, though, Ignatius will usually suggest appropriate affections for the colloquy; he rarely puts precise words on the retreatant's lips. Though the fundamental trustworthiness of profound faithful love can be predicted, love's intensity of emotion and articulation of words cannot always be foretold. So the precise emotional tone and words of the heart's colloquy will be more spontaneously affected both by the consolations that further, and by the desolations that resist, the growing interpersonal intimacy of Ignatian contemplation. The colloquy born of these consolations and desolations organically prepares for a prayer of repetition[15] and then can gradually become a profound composure of heart unifying the souls of lovers in a wordless quiet that radiates in the eyes and in gentle touch. In this way, Ignatian contemplation, in a manner true of all mature love, finally leads to such careful, thorough coalescence as to have become not only dialogue but duet.

Ignatian Contemplation and Presence in the World

As a process of interpersonal assimilation to God, Ignatian contemplation is first and foremost an end unto itself; then, and only then, is it also a means to special apostolic presence in the world. As we have seen so far, all the elements of Ignatian contemplation aim at one thing: a thorough and intimate being with and in God. As lovers know, being with the beloved is such a paramount and supreme value that it needs no further justification. Therefore, whether it be contemplation of the love of friendship, to overlook its value as an end in itself, to be too utilitarian about it as a means to something else, betrays only a surface experience both of contemplation and of the friendship of lovers.

Nevertheless, though Ignatian contemplation is primarily a companionship in love, because it is such a profound companionship, it does have a definite secondary side-effect. The intimate experience of the awesome mystery of a loving God in all the details of Jesus gives special vision to the eyes of the soul and a vigorous touch to the hands and fingers of an active presence in the world. Contemplation, where allowed to weld a profound inner composure of love, will fashion an apostolic, worldly presence of gifted sensitivity—that is, contemplative, loving faith ineluctably promotes loving servants of justice.

This special, active apostolic presence is the result of the interplay of mystery and history in Ignatian contemplation. The contemplations of the Incarnation and the Nativity at the beginning of the Second Week serve as models for this interplay and gradual interpenetration of the awesome mystery of God's love with the touching historical human details of Jesus of Nazareth. In the Incarnation, there is a movement from the heart of sheer mystery, in the Trinity's loving decision, to the history and earthly details of a Jewish girl's overwhelming annunciation experience. Here, mystery moves to flesh in history whereas in the Nativity contemplation, the dynamic shifts. There, we are invited to enter very immediately and emotionally as a participant into the historical details of an uprooted young Jewish girl's giving birth in a foreign setting:[16] surely, a rather ordinary and not infrequent scene in those days. By taking the details very seriously, by

cherishing them in faith, we pass through to, and finally
kneel in, reverent wonder before the astonishing mystery of
a dear God laboring for and loving us to the very end. It is
like the process of some contemporary Christologies that
take the humanity of Jesus very seriously and find there the
awesome mysteriousness of divinity. The movement here
is through history into mystery. And through the remaining
three weeks of the Exercises, in each Gospel scene of Jesus,
we experience this interplay of mystery and history moving
toward interpretation:

> Notice here a twofold affective, contemplative dialectic:
> from mystery to history, from history to mystery—
> pressing ever toward the full, rich experience of mystery
> in history, history *as* mystery (full Incarnation become
> now not merely a faith-fact, or doctrine, but faith-*experience*).[17]

This contemplative experience of careful interpretation
of mystery and history gradually has its influence in the busy
arena of daily life. An apostolic soul develops special vision;
apostolic senses have fine tuning. In the tangled activity of
daily life, by seriously treasuring all the details of *this* time and
this place, and precisely by *not* escaping the circumstances and
options of the here and now, we can find and taste and smell
and touch a God, mysteriously and wonderfully laboring and
loving to the end. Contemplation's discovery of the interpretation of mystery and history allows an apostolic acknowledgement in daily life of the same dynamic fusion of detailed
earthly history and awesome Divine mystery. The continuing
rhythm of formal contemplation and action moves the apostle to an integration and special presence in action as prayer.

It is, then, a daily mysticism of careful, detailed service that grows out of the process of Ignatian contemplation.

Ignatian contemplation is a school of discernment. A mysticism of pilgrim service is the daily incarnation of a discernment learned in contemplation and now giving a special presence in the world. To seek out and freely respond to the breath and fingerprints of God in every situation is very different from a life either of doing whatever one wants or of a secularly competent but spiritually naïve commitment. The contemplations of the Second Week create an inner milieu and atmosphere of heart within which confusion, doubt, and cowardice gradually evanesce as decisions emerge with a clarity, courage, and energy for action. The invitation of God, even when it involves anguished suffering and frustrating hardship, as Jesus knew in that darksome olive grove, can hearken with an enlightening attractiveness that is almost irresistible. This milieu of heart, this profound inner orientation to God, is the lover's experiential feel for a beloved God's truth recognized here and now in a way that is not simply the result of syllogistic reasoning.

This intuitive sense for the beloved's way and desire has important implications for the role of contemplation in relation to the Two Standards and the Election in the Exercises. Since this inner contemplative composure is just beginning to develop, Ignatius has us spend a whole day meditating on the Two Standards. While, at first, it may seem an interruption to a simple contemplative style of prayer, this meditation, after four successive hours of prayer, itself coalesces as part of the growing inner composure. It is no slip of the pen when Ignatius later refers to the Two Standards as a "contemplation."[18] Four hours of prayer have given the meditation a simple but very enlightening contemplative presence in one's heart and consciousness. And now, this enlightened consciousness becomes a backdrop to be further sharpened and discovered in the ongoing contemplative investigation and receiving of Jesus during the retreat. Beyond the retreat, it continues as a focus synchronizing a human heart to the mentality and way of God in Jesus and inspiring courageous apostolic interpretation and service of God's way in all the cultural worldly particulars of daily life. One lives and loves and serves now carefully and gratefully, but always in light of the cosmic confrontation between the two standards.

This inner atmosphere of heart enlightened in the vision of the Two Standards then focuses the election, whether it be of a state in life or something less comprehensive. As contemplative intimacy with Jesus grows and as we surrender to the attractiveness of God's loving way in Jesus, we can recognize, receive, and choose the specific details, whatever they may be, of that way for us now. This recognition is not usually dramatic and instantaneous. Rather, it can be a gradual dawning carefully discerned. Nor is it restricted to the special time of retreat. In the midst of busy life, these specific invitations will be recognized. But one thing is sure: without this inner contemplative composure, the particular vocation will be neither recognized nor followed with appropriate reverence and seriousness.

Conclusion

In summary, then, both the method of Ignatian prayer in general and the specifics of contemplation in the Second Week of the Exercises are meant to facilitate the interpersonal encounter and union of a human person with God.

Far beyond any earthly realization on our part, God is always laboring in every human heart to initiate the contemplative process of luring us into a whole new spirit of life and love in Jesus. Contemplation plays a major role in our acknowledging and living our true identity: a consoling companionship, not only in prayer but in all of life, with God lovingly faithful, even on Calvary, to and in Jesus, beyond any power of this world. What greater tragedy in life could there be than utter lack of awareness of this glory promised and available to each of us? Through contemplation, we truly become whom we contemplate and whom we are all meant to be. For, whether we realize it or not, it is in God's love, and in our loving response in prayer and service, that we live and move and have our selves.

NOTES

1. Joseph Whelan, "Jesuit Apostolic Prayer" in *The Way* (Supplement) 19 (1973): 18. This whole article's brief, very concentrated treatment of Ignatian method in prayer has been very provocative of my own development here.

2. William Johnston, *The Inner Eye of Love* (San Francisco: Harper, 1978), 29.

3. Goncalves DaCámara, *Memoriale*, p. 256, in *Scripta de Sancto Ignatio*, 1, p. 278.

4. Gerard Manley Hopkins, "As Kingfishers Catch Fire."

5. Karl Rahner, *Spiritual Exercises* (New York: Herder and Herder, 1965), 114-115.

6. See *The Spiritual Exercises of Saint Ignatius of Loyola*, 73-75.

7. See *Spiritual Exercises*, 46.

8. See Psalm 17:8.

9. William Peters, *The Spiritual Exercises of St. Ignatius* (Jersey City: Program To Adapt the Spiritual Exercises, 1968), 22-24.

10. See *Spiritual Exercises*, 107.

11. Peters, 35, 26.

12. Ibid., 22-24.

13. See *Spiritual Exercises*, 114.

14. See *Spiritual Exercises*, 116.

15. See *Spiritual Exercises*, 118.

16. Mary is already displaced (she is from Nazareth) in the flight into Egypt; the Matthean theology will find her actually a refugee.

17. Joseph Whelan, 17.

18. See *Spiritual Exercises*, 156.

MONASTICISM OF THE HEART
THE CORE OF ALL CHRISTIAN LIFESTYLES

When detached from a radical experience of oneself as alone with God, the two lifestyles of apostolic action[1] and vowed monasticism become superficial, simply a matter of externals. Some of the qualities of the two lifestyles can be considered both "as a profound inner reality of heart and as an external expression of that same interior reality."[2] If there is not a profound inner reality of heart, the two lifestyles become superficial, competitive, and even misleading.

The monastic way of life and the active way of life can, at times, be ranked in a priority that reveals more competition than mutual understanding. This competitive mentality always belies a failure to appreciate the one and only necessary foundation—what this essay is calling the monasticism of the heart—that undergirds any and all different Christian spiritualities—that is, ways of living. When an unhealthy spirit of comparison comes into play, then the monastic and apostolic lifestyles influence one another illegitimately. An active vocation, for example, can be distrusted because of monastic expectations and evaluation. But in these days of special urgency for direct, immediate service in our needy world, the greater danger might be the monastic life's becoming too actively oriented. There are different inner motive forces at work in each lifestyle. When well understood, these different motive forces and the different patterns of life they create can promote and validate the distinctiveness of these two lifestyles and, therefore, can be very helpful in discerning an individual's vocation to one or the other. These two dynamics, when perceived for what they are, allow an interaction that is enriching and not confusing or destructive of the basic identities involved.

But these two monastic and active dynamics of external lifestyle must always be profoundly rooted in one and the same experience of being alone with God. I am naming this foundational experience "monasticism of the heart." This ontological, psychological, affective monasticism, deep in the heart and beyond any lifestyle, is a core religious experience that must ground the identity of all serious disciples of Jesus Christ. Though it must be carefully distinguished from an external monastic lifestyle—for we are speaking of a different thing—this monasticism of the heart anchors Christian identity in an experience of God far beyond anything of this world and it, thereby, stands forth as the absolutely essential foundation for both the active and the monastic lifestyles. Though the Greek word *monos* historically developed some further aspects of its meaning, especially along communitarian lines with Eusebius and Augustine into the fourth and fifth centuries, nonetheless, the word's basic meaning continues to signify an aloneness, a solitariness.[3] The experience I am describing is one that strips and purifies, scours the heart to a radical solitude of aloneness in and with God. For this reason, monasticism of the heart, rather than confusing the

issue, seems an appropriate depiction of the experience presented here.

Jesus' Calvary experience, while starkly enmeshed in the
worldly details of His time, dramatically exposes His own
deepest identity as lovingly absorbed in an invisible "dear
Father," experienced as far greater than this world. This
exemplary experience of Jesus, beginning at least with Baptism, becomes an invitation for all serious disciples to a fundamental re-announcement of their lives that shifts and roots
their identity center in a radical experience of God alone.

Jesus' Calvary Experience

At the Last Supper, on the night before He died, Jesus is
seized by a moment of special, explicit awareness, as John's
Gospel records it. Jesus knew "that the Father had put everything into his power and that he had come from God and
was returning to God . . . " (Jn 13:3). It is the awareness of a
man who has decided, in the face of opposition hardened in
the decision to kill Him, to enter the darkness of threatened
death and to stand lovingly and firmly for the truth—something to which the ministry of His whole life had led Him,
and now simply demanded of Him. He could not, he would
not, back off the issue. And the issue was surely more than
something worldly; it was more than some question of
human success or the defense of some human ideology.
Though it would have enormously important repercussions
for the whole world, the issue reached far beyond anything
then and there.

The ministry of Jesus' life had implicated Him with the
joys and sorrows, the success and failure, the daily details of
weakness and neediness in the lives of women and men who

were rich and poor, publicly influential and privately hidden. The Word of God became unquestionably human and shared profoundly the concerns of His people. The compassion of His heart and the touch of His hand restored hope, healed affliction, and renewed life. And yet, in some way, He was not His own master. "The words I speak to you I do not speak on my own. The Father who dwells in me is doing his works. Believe me that I am in the Father and the Father is in me" (Jn 14:10-11).

From that day when Jesus was led away from His home in Nazareth and was given over by His mother to a more public ministry, His heart, His consciousness, His whole being was caught up and at home with someone who always seemed so intimately close and yet far beyond the details, or the sum, of any daily situation. At the Jordan, as His sensitivity identified Him with all sinful people everywhere, His baptismal experience confirmed a dear Father's choice of Him in a love and favor that extroverted His heart in breathless wonder, prayer, and expectant zeal. And temptation, all through His life, tested and revealed the depth and durability of that love and favor in the face of this world's threatening, seductive designs. It is clear: in some profound way, He is not his own. He is a Son whose whole being utterly relies on his Father—always and only, fully at home with that dear Father.

This at-homeness with the Father gives an urgency and intensity to Jesus' ministry among the people. Isaiah foretold him: "Upon him I have put my spirit; he shall bring forth justice to the nations" (Is 42:1). His compassionate spirit allows Him to become identified with the struggles of His people in a great desire that God's loving justice be revealed and accomplished. This urgent direction in His life provokes opposition among some of the people and leads to the show-down that now faces him. And He cannot back down. He knows "he is returning to God." It is the lure and invitation of His dear Father's love that made possible at the deepest center of His being the choice of His Death as a choice for love and for life. And that is why at the Last Supper with His friends, this moment of special awareness and courage prompts a symbolic gesture of self-emptying love and service: He washes their feet.

This gesture of perfect love (Jn 13:1) symbolizes the meaning of Jesus' whole past life, and even more especially, it symbolizes His coming, final experience on Calvary when He is lifted beyond the point of any return. Strengthened in an olive grove's fearful, anguished renewal of obedient abandonment of self into the providential loving hands of his Father, He literally gives Himself over into the hands of His adversaries. But for a moment in that olive grove, the imminent prospect of death strikes savagely, violently at the sensibleness of human reason. No temporal cause or rationale, no human ideology brings saving significance into that moment's temporary absurdity. Only a dear Father's love and a mission transcending all ages and boundaries brings light into such darkness. "Do not let your hearts be troubled . . . if I go and prepare a place for you, I will come back again and take you to myself, so that where I am you also may be" (Jn 14:1-3).

The composure of such at-homeness with His Father carries Jesus through all the isolating and cruelly humiliating details of suffering in His Passion and Way of the Cross. All along that way, and not only of this last journey to Calvary, but also of the last months of His life, He is stripped of various supports. "As a result of this, many [of] his disciples returned to their former way of life and no longer accompanied him" (Jn 6:66). And then, after being physically stripped of His clothes and lifted on the Cross, a last, far starker stripping occurred. Having always been composed with and energized by such a loving Father's favor and choice, Jesus now feels Himself forsaken and, at the level of *experience*, utterly separated from that Father who has always been there for Him, though at the profoundest level of *being* Son, He remains never more united: the only Son of a most faithful Father. In that moment of final, intense testing, Jesus believes in, reclaims, and has confirmed for Himself, what has always been His home and the center of His identity: a loving Father faithful beyond earthly imagining. Because it is absolutely all He has left in this moment of apparent forsakenness, His true and only home stands out dramatically.

Stretched out on the Cross between heaven and earth, Jesus not only gathers and concentrates in His heart, like a laser beam, all the reality and love of God, but then also, and very importantly, like a prism, His heart disperses that love in a way that can enlighten our vision of the whole universe. The deepest composure of His heart, focused wordlessly on His dear Father, announces His center of identity with rock-like hope: "My soul rests in God alone, from whom comes my salvation. God alone is my rock and salvation, my fortress; I shall never fall. . . . My soul be at rest in God alone, from whom comes my hope" (Ps 62:2-3, 6). And that rock-like hope beyond any sensible, felt experience is blessed by His dear Father with the response of Resurrection. But this victory of God in the heart of Jesus on Calvary, stripping and purifying Him of any reliance on an earthly hope as ultimately invincible, is not some escape or turning away

from the world. Rather, the glorious victory consummated
in the crucified One is a saving mystery of renewed life and
love and hope stretching limitlessly throughout the universe
into the fullness of time. It is an explosion of the Holy Spirit
bringing new, joyous freedom and energetic enthusiasm into
hearts, for the renewal of the face of the earth. Salvador
Dali's painting of "Christ of St. John of the Cross" is one
artistic example that catches the renewed vision of the world
that radiates from the heart of Jesus crucified.

Christian Identity

The experience on Calvary that strips the heart of Jesus
of all tangible earthly support and leaves Him with God alone
exposes His most profound identity. That radical aloneness
of Jesus in and with His dear Father, that profound monasticism of the heart, also points the way for anyone serious
about discipleship of Jesus Christ. To discover rock-like hope
beyond any fear of failure responds to the deepest longing
of all our hearts—for we are made in His image. And so it is
revealed in Jesus' own experience; all Christian piety is a piety
of the Cross.[4] Across the centuries, therefore, pilgrims have
known where to go—to the Holy Land; and they have stood,
knelt, and sat there, in touch not only with the skull-like rock
of Calvary, but also with the saving experience of the One
crucified there for all. Though it is never easy to remain long
enough in contemplation of the mystery of Calvary, Christian women and men of all ages have found in that radical
simplicity and aloneness—at times, to their own surprise,
consolation. Yes, beyond the fright and fear of such cruel suffering resonates a consolation that can withstand any and all
trials in life. Christian piety always focuses in contemplation

of the Cross, and all its generous service radiates from that profound and faithful center of identity.

Sharing Jesus' experience of Calvary can happen in many different ways. For some people, a catastrophe suddenly stretches their heart to the length of God. On the pinnacle of such a peak experience, the twin challenge of the apparent absurdity of life and the refuge of a God greater than this world's absurdity seems anything but ordinary; it is breath- lessly sensational. The critical choice is stark and clear. The outcome is equally clear and crucial: despair in absurdity or hope in renewed life. For other people, the stakes are just as costly, but the experience is much more ordinary, much less dramatic. The stretching of their hearts to the length of God happens only gradually and over time. The beauty of God's love shining forth in the details of this world may only slowly fascinate their hearts in a contemplation that also only slowly intimates a mysterious fullness beckoning beyond present experience.

Whether this foundational experience of reliance on God alone happens in an excitingly critical way or in a quiet, ordinary way, it almost never happens all at once—that is, in such a profound way that it takes root for a lifetime. Rather, it grows and develops only over years, even a whole lifetime. And so, this monasticism of the heart, rather than established in one specific experience, whether peak or ordinary, is rather an orientation in faith whose development takes time. Nonetheless, as a foundational dynamic essential to Christian discipleship, it always shakes any previous identity and estab- lishes a new person in Christ. This developing dynamic, this fundamental orientation in faith, cannot be bypassed without forfeiting some important qualities that are necessary, but not easy today, for Christian service in the world: durability, faithfulness, and hope-filled joy. Since the development of this dynamic in faith is never automatic, it requires a choice of cooperation on our part. And it always costs a radical conversion of our whole person. This choice and conversion, initiated and empowered in Baptism, stretches over our whole lifetime.

Baptismal Re-announcement

At the very center of baptismal empowerment is a radical re-announcement of this identity. Christian baptismal experience implies a belief in God's love so powerfully manifest in the raising of Jesus as to gainsay any final defeat and, therefore, as capable of transforming an apostle's shuddering fear into a humbly confident peace and a zealous hope. But smuggled within baptismal faith and always ready to invite us beyond ourselves lurks a moment of stark choice: a God whose love conquers all absurdity or a world whose beauty in and of itself, finally, is absurdly chimerical and unpredictable. Such a choice is not, first and foremost, a matter of our own effort. It is a choice revealed and made for us and with us in the graced beauty of Jesus Christ, especially in His Calvary experience. Jesus Himself has made this choice, not just for Himself, but also for each of us. It is a choice of God, of God alone, as a love far beyond all other loves and, alone, fully satisfying for our restless hearts.

Though this choice is primarily made for us in Jesus Christ, it is a choice that must be confirmed by us all in the fundamental re-announcement of our whole identity in faith. In Baptism, the whole identity of our experience shifts.[5] Through Christ, our identity now focuses in a dear

God, lovely and attractive beyond worldly comparison. And so, Baptism, as it initiates in our hearts this monastic experience of God alone, involves in some careful, real way a renunciation of this world with all its goodness and all its allurements—precisely a renunciation of it as our identity center. As baptized, we stand in Christ, identified finally and fully in God alone. Only God's love in Christ, creatively and faithfully giving life into the fullness of time, provides ultimate assurance.

But this baptismal identity-shift, while rooted in a decisive choice of God over the world, does not produce an irresponsible negation of any beauty and value in the world. In fact, the re-announcement described here has precisely the opposite effect. To have had our identity stretched beyond our selfish limits into the fullness of God's faithful love and, therefore, to have renounced the world as one's identity center is not to lose the world. Rather, it reveals a whole new vision of the world: as belonging to God redeemed in the mystery of Christ—and with the Holy Spirit daily struggling to radiate the grandeur of God's reconciling love within the infinite variety of human affairs. And all those alight with the fire of God's love in the quiet intimacy of their hearts simply must be part of this radiant daily struggle in the Holy Spirit. Any diffident suspicion of the world is transformed, therefore, in the enlightening love radiating from the heart of the crucified Christ fully abandoned to His Father and blessed in the gift of Resurrection. To contemplate Jesus on the Cross is, finally, not to hold back, but to be propelled into the mission of the Spirit. Jesus' words in the Gospel of John become a realized prophecy and issue a clarion call of enlightened confident zeal: "Now is the time of judgement on this world;

now the ruler of this world will be driven out. And when I am lifted up from the earth, I will draw everyone to myself" (Jn 12:31-32).

From God to World

The revelation of God in the experience of Jesus always points the way for all His disciples. Just as Jesus came, *sent* from the heart of the Trinity into the world, so the Christian is always sent into the world in the context of a special experience alone with God. From God into the world—not in the reverse order. The ontological movement fundamental to Christian spirituality rooted in the Cross is from God into the world—and it cannot be reversed without serious repercussions. To blur the decisive privacy of God's love in our hearts is always to blur the clarity of our perception of the world as belonging to God. It is precisely the transcendent, eschatological reality of God's infinitely creative love that founds and makes possible the absolutely universal, incarnational presence of Jesus Christ in our world. J.M.R. Tillard, O.P., makes the same point strongly and clearly: "Why become involved in the world then? . . . On account of God and of what Jesus Christ is for the believer, not principally or fundamentally on account of human solidarity. The 'not of the world' quality is the driving force of the 'in the world' quality . . . Having its roots in a familiarity with God, and not first and foremost in human solidarity, is what gives to Christian involvement its special character and shape."[6]

And so, if prejudice and unbelief shrink our experience of God's transcendent reality, then we cannot discover the incarnational presence of Christ in much of a universal way. Until we experience all things as found in God, we will not, and we cannot, find God in all things. But in an age infatuated with incarnational immediacy, the transcendent, eschatological dimensions of reality can seem vaguely unreal, like an escape into abstraction. But it is faith precisely in the transcendent mystery of God's love infinite beyond any other love that can give enthusiasm, freedom, hope, and joy to our hearts in every incarnational situation of our universe.

This total loving reliance on God alone, often described in extraordinary mystical experiences, must underlie the daily loving service of all disciples of Jesus Christ. This experience of loving reliance on God alone, purified of any temporal image and support over years, has purified many mystical souls in the trial of dark, painful faith and has extroverted them in speechless adoration. But such purifying and adoring reliance on God alone is not meant only for extraordinary mystics. This purifying adoration pierces to the very core of Christian faith and, therefore, responds to the deepest longing of every human heart. "My soul rests in God alone" (Ps 62:1). Fr. Tillard again points out how crucial such adoration is for busy apostles. "Our trouble arises from our becoming involved in the world without adoring God... it is adoration—the total recognition of God's gift by heart and mind—which is the nurturing womb without which nothing viable can be born."[7] Such adoring reliance on God alone is motivated by and experience of God's love that is far more than ordinary. But it is not reserved for only a few privileged souls. Being stretched in love to the length of God is a privilege to which grace inclines all serious believers. It identifies their hearts in nothing less than the fullness of God's love revealed and promised in Christ. It is this experience as it grows and stretches over a lifetime that becomes at once a

metaphysical and a deeply devout monasticism of the heart—
a monasticism whose precise meaning here is a necessary, full
component of, while differentiated from, both the monastic
and the active Christian lifestyles.

Some Examples

This choice of God and this reliance on God alone
beyond all else, this monasticism of the heart, in the long history of Christian spirituality has fashioned the lives of many
men and women according to the inspiration of Jesus' own
example. Mary, the woman chosen to play, in God's saving
love, the uniquely special role of being at once first disciple
and greatest of all saints, surely knew the experience of total
reliance in faith on God alone beyond the evidence of natural
understanding and certitude. From beginning to end, she is
the handmaid of the Lord, belonging to Him body and soul,
and ready for whatever He desires. From the Annunciation
to the relieved finding in the temple, and in many other painful situations in the public life of her Son, she is most likely
quite stripped, on the natural level, of comprehension and
left standing, therefore, in an appalling, most beautiful, naked
faith. On Calvary, this handmaid of the Lord stands in the
face of what all senses and all reason declare to be darkness
and destruction, starkly exulting in God her savior, alone with
the One whose name is holy and who will help—mercy being
above all His works. She will know one further, quite final
standing by.

With a simplicity typical of his whole converted life, "My
God and my all," Francis of Assisi's favorite prayer, expresses
a total concentration of his being in a God whose love alone
fully satisfied his heart.[8] And yet, this pointed focus of his

whole heart on God made possible the intensely incarnational witness and love of his life. And so, it is enormously signifi-cant that only after La Verna, after Jesus' Calvary experience had seared itself into Francis's flesh, only then could this frail, fiery troubadour pour out "The Canticle of Brother Sun" in praise of God's beautiful love everywhere in creation.[9]

A half century later, a similar realization of the decisive primacy of God's love brought Thomas Aquinas to an abrupt halt and left unfinished the tremendous accomplishments of his life. In 1273 after Mass, he returned strangely altered to his work on *Summa Theologiae*. This landmark contribu-tion to Christian thought stops almost in mid-sentence as he declares, "All I have written seems to me nothing but straw . . . compared to what I have seen and what has been revealed to me."[10]

Ignatius of Loyola, more than two centuries later, in a prayer of abandonment summarizing the whole development of the *Spiritual Exercises,* says much the same to God, "Take, Lord, receive . . . Give me your love and your grace, for this is sufficient for me."[11] And Ignatius also knew clearly that only insofar as he was stretched to the fullness of God whose love overshadows all other love and, therefore, only insofar as he was well enough mortified in all things his whole life become a grateful service to the Divine Majesty present and self-giving in absolutely everything.

In the seventeenth century, Mary Ward, strongly influ-enced by Ignatius's vision as she founded the Institute of the Blessed Virgin Mary, demonstrated the same lively belief in her absolute reliance on God's transcendent love. This belief allowed her to find, in a severe mortification of her selfish-ness, God's providential love when enormous, shocking trials and suffering seemed to present her with so much evidence to the contrary. Her beloved Institute suppressed, for all practical purposes imprisoned in a convent in Munich and deprived of the sacraments for nine weeks, she gave graceful expression to her reliance on God's gentle love alone: "Our Lord and Master is also our Father and gives no more than ladylike and what is most easy to be borne."[12]

Mary Ward's example of monasticism of the heart is matched in the lives of other women whose profound reliance on God alone was tested by the painful misunderstanding of their own apostolically active charism and the active charism of the congregations they struggled to found—for example, Angela Merici, Louise de Marillac, Marguerite Bourgeoys. And beyond the examples given here, the lives of many men and women, religious and lay, each in their own way, reveal a strength found in God alone, a strength that overcomes fierce obstacles in the desire to do great things for God in service of the people.

Renewed and Kept Effective

After this monasticism of the heart experience has taken effect profoundly enough in someone's life, two further questions surface: How can we keep this experience alive? What are some of the practical results in our lives that will demonstrate the liveliness and effectiveness of this experience?

After we know the experience of being stretched wide open in surrender to God's faithful love, a foundation has been laid that reveals itself in some practical results in our lives. And when such an abandonment has forged a deep peace in our hearts, the concern then quickly arises of keeping such a foundational experience alive and operative. It is

easy—in fact, it is usually the expected inclination of our
hearts—for this special experience to fade and fail over time.
And in its failing, not only do our hearts begin to shrink, but
the consequences of such and experience of surrender alone
with God also begin to dim. Though it is the very nature of
our human hearts to long for self-transcendence through
self-abandonment, still we all know the strong, though often
unconsciously insidious, tendency to live a more controlled,
predictable life, constricted by selfish, easily rationalized and
justified personal preference and prejudice.

Without regular reflection, the radically abandoned heart
easily slips back into a more self-enclosed orientation to life.
Consciousness examen can deflect this: a daily reflection
whereby we carefully notice the contour of our hearts, renew
in gratitude the expansiveness of God's love for us, and
honestly repent of limited responses to such love in the specific details of the day. Such regular examen helps us at first
to recognize, then to prevent or be converted from, those
constrictive maneuvers of a subtly self-enclosing heart. Such
reflection also keeps us sensitive to those concrete moments
in our loving service of others in which God invites us to
a renewed surrender beyond self that always extroverts our
hearts in loving, confident reliance on Jesus Christ, God's
great, faithful promise for the fullness of time. Such invitations from God's love to step beyond narrow self-defined
limits are always addressed to us. God's jealous desires for the
full surrender of our hearts in love never cease.

Daily Eucharist also provides regular, awesome opportunity to renew monasticism of the heart. Gathered in faith,
and prayerfully receiving that sharp, loving word of God that
judges secret emotions and thoughts, we are challenged to

the radical act of trust that Eucharist is. Far beyond any celebration simply of ourselves or our local concerns, however
valuable they may be, Eucharist places us at the center of all
time and within the fullness of all reality in Jesus' full-hearted,
self-emptying response to His dear Father's love at the Last
Supper and on Calvary. Eucharistic love is judgment, tearing
the curtain from our hearts, stretching our heart's love to the
lengths of God alone—and to the breadth of Divine care
for this world. Such a regular experience of God's infinitely
expansive love does not overlook the daily concerns of our
hearts. But by restoring them to an enlarged perspective,
it allows us to inhale a hope that is renewing, relaxing, and
inspiringly energetic, too.

Renewed in Solitude

Without a doubt, the most important means, under God's
grace, for renewing and keeping alive monasticism of the
heart is regular time alone in the solitude of God's love. This
experience of solitude can take a great variety of expressions.
Sometimes private, secret acts of penance and asceticism
root us deeply in contemplative solitude and symbolize our
standing alone in a full reliance on God's love for us that will
always baffle and convict the secular spirit of the age. Sometimes, in our contemporary world, another kind of penance
and asceticism must more publicly witness for God against
specific secular issues. But these acts of penance, whether
hidden and undramatic or publicly demonstrated, if based in
a contemplative context, bespeak an identity stretched to the
length of God alone and enthusiastically alive in service of
this world.

At other times, solitude takes the form of a more
extended time of prayer alone with God. Whether it is a
daily protracted time of personal prayer alone or a monthly
hermitage-day or some other regular time of quiet recollection, the issue is always the same: to stop all busy activity and
just *be*, alone, in the profound peace and quiet of God's love.
Most often, this is not easy but calls us up short and shakes
us free of life's many urgent concerns so as to expose and
renew the one truly important reality in life: full, trusting obedience to God's saving love in Jesus Christ.[13] In *The Way of
the Heart*, Henri Nouwen calls solitude the necessary furnace
of transformation whereby the compulsive minister becomes
more and more compassionate.[14] This scorching purification of our many compulsions burns its way patiently and
gradually into the deep center of our hearts where each of us
stands, lives, and breathes, in and with God alone. In this way,
solitude confronts and invites each and all of us, beyond any
introvert-extrovert distinction, to a monasticism of the heart
that roots our identity in the Trinity of God, and at a depth
of heart beneath all external, active, and monastic lifestyles.

In this profound ontological monasticism of the heart,
the two apostolic lifestyles of the monastic and the active, as
different as they are, find a common grounding and identity.
Michael Buckley, in rooting the Jesuit qualities of missionary
availability and "finding God in all things" in profound solitude, is really describing a dynamic that must be true in some
way for all active disciples of the Lord.

For Ignatius, there had to be something profoundly
eremitical about the Jesuit, something self-contained
and independent so that he can move from place to

place, from work to work, from house to house. This
absolute detachment from *stabilitas*, from the definition
of his life within a particular place or church or group,
radically distinguished the Jesuit from either the monk or
the hermit, but it was a detachment which was possible
only if there was something strongly solitary about his
spirituality. Paradoxically, this "eremitical" element made
apostolic availability possible. There has always been
subsequently something "alone" about the Jesuit, and
if this solitude is not to dwarf his affectivity it is only
because he has found God within this aloneness. . . .
Not even Bruno himself asserted this interdependence
between solitude, detachment, and the finding of God
more starkly than Ignatius.[15]

St. Bruno, the founder of the Carthusians, "was wholly
engaged in choosing God alone in every circumstance and
absolutely."[16] Ignatius of Loyola chose—God chose in him—
the same focus for his heart.[17] And though the externals of
the Carthusian and Jesuit lifestyles vary substantively, as the
monastic and active always should and do, still Bruno and
Ignatius are soul brothers in responding to what this essay
seeks to focus on and name—our common call to monasticism of the heart.

Results

This monastic experience central to all serious Christian
discipleship not only contains within itself a particular vision
of the world, it also produces clear signs of the liveliness
and effectiveness of this profound rooting of our hearts
in God's love alone. Some of these results are qualities that
seem in short supply today. In the face of undeserved and

unexplained suffering, of bitter and revengeful hatred, of unjust and enslaving poverty, apostolic hope, joy, and enthusiasm seem naively unrealistic, if not absolutely impossible. Disillusionment and despondency verging on angry despair can seem understandable inhabitants in the hearts of some apostles active in our world. Only one profoundly rooted and ultimately identified in God beyond the world becomes enlightened enough to recognize God's suffering, saving love at work throughout the universe and, then, becomes free and faithful enough to commit oneself to God's passionately loving justice revealed in the mystery of Christ crucified to the fullness of Resurrection. It is only through such an experience that one can come to an indefatigable hope, joy, and enthusiasm, whatever may happen. The lack of such qualities will always limit the Church's missionary response to specific critical needs. But even worse, it will corrupt and gainsay our witness to the Good News of a God whose love has a power to save and transform this world beyond the interference of any worldly power.

In this way, the finding and serving of God is not limited to personal prejudice but extends as far and wide as God's universal saving love in the mystery of Christ. And so, light and darkness, life and death, success and failure, just and unjust situations, a ministry I like and one for which I seem not very fitted: none of these, nor any of countless other alternatives, become either-or choices about God's loving presence, but rather both-and situations confidently and faithfully revealing the mystery of God's universally saving love in Christ to generous, insightful, free apostles—pacified and strengthened, surely, in the support of one another, but finally, in a hope against hope about God's love alone.

Without a genuine monasticism of the heart, however, such insightful apostolic vision, enthusiastic freedom, and unquenchably joyous hope are simply not possible. The courage of human willpower alone is certainly not even at issue here. Rather, the issue is faith—faith acted out as relationship—a faith that can move the mountains of disbelief in our own hearts and reveal to those chosen the attractiveness of God's superabundant love standing strong in our weakness.

This monastic experience, as it strips our hearts more and more of prejudice and overly protective self-defense, will lead to cumulative, foundational experiences of identity in the paschal mystery of Christ crucified, such that God's love stands forth everywhere in everything. A God whose saving love is doubtlessly at work in all things can actually be found in all things, but only by the person faithfully purified in the experience of the *monos*—the experience of being with God alone. For this person, though, all life, however plain, humdrum, or even incongruous, becomes religious experience. The sacred-secular split in human experience that often saps the energy of our hearts can thus be healed in an integration that discovers and focuses God's loving grace and then finds a body for God's Spirit, present in all human experience.

My own experience, personal and vicarious, suggests that we will and should continue to struggle to recognize the active and the monastic as two equally valid apostolic lifestyles. But even more importantly, as this article seeks to make clear, we need to recognize contemporary invitations to a monasticism of the heart which roots us in Jesus Christ and without which neither of these two apostolic lifestyles can escape fragmentation, rootlessness, and that final disappointment which simply must come to any life whose ultimate identity, in its depth and solitude, is not the indwelling Trinity of God alone (see Jn 14:23). The fundamental monastic invitation which has been under discussion here is addressed to us all. And it reveals to all of us at once the attractive fullness of a dear God's love beyond all earthly imagining; the restlessly expansive nature of our hearts, never ultimately satisfied in this world; and, finally, the saving mystery of Christ passionately alive in the Spirit and eager to absorb all our energies in the exhilarating renewal of the face of or earth into the fullness of time. Paul gives flame and force to this, our most fundamental truth in glorious, bold language a hundred different ways, all of them generative of a great apostolic zeal. Here are just two: "your true life is a hidden one in God, through Christ" (Col 3:3) and "I still live my human life, but it is a life of faith in the Son of God, who loved me and gave himself for me" (Ga 2:20). This is monasticism of the heart.

NOTES

1. My use of the phrase "apostolic action" does not simply refer to some religious congregations. It can also refer to marriage and the single life.
2. *Review for Religious* (September-October 1986), 658.
3. See Kenneth Leech, *True God* (London: Sheldon Press, 1985), 142 and the following pages.
4. See Karl Rahner, "Ignatian Mysticism of Joy in the World," *Theological Investigations* 3 (London: Darton, Longman, & Todd, 1967), 281-283.
5. See Romans 6:8-11 for clarity of how Baptism changes the whole identity of our experience.
6. J. M. R. Tillard, O.P., *Dilemmas of Modern Religious Life* (Wilmington: Michael Glazier, Inc., 1984), 52-53.
7. Ibid., 50. On the same page, Fr. Tillard has an even stronger warning: "Working *in the world*, bravely sharing in the efforts to bring about liberation—these are truly evangelical if carried out *before* God and in a spirit of adoration. Otherwise not."
8. See Murray Bodo, O.F.M., *The Way of St. Francis* (New York: Image, 1985), 75.
9. Ibid., 143-151.
10. See Josef Pieper, *The Silence of St. Thomas* (New York: Pantheon, 1957), 39-40.
11. Louis J. Puhl, ed., *The Spiritual Exercises* (Westminster, MD: Newman Press, 1959), sec. 234.
12. Deidre Rofe, "Journey into Freedom," *The Way Supplement* 53 (Summer 1985): 11.
13. See Henri Nouwen, *The Road to Daybreak* (New York: Doubleday, 1988), 81-23, for treatment of distinction between what is urgent and what is important.
14. See Henri Nouwen, *The Way of the Heart* (New York: Seabury, 1981), 19-40.
15. Michael Buckley, S.J., "Mission in Companionship: of Jesuit Community and Communion," *Studies in the Spirituality of Jesuits* 2, no. 4, 15.
16. Jean Leclerq, Francis Vandenbrouche, Louis Bouyer, *A History of Christian Spirituality*, Vol. II: *Spirituality of the Middle Ages* (New York: Crossroad, 1968), 151.
17. See *The Constitutions of the Society of Jesus*, George E. Ganss, S.J., ed. (St. Louis: Institute of Jesuit Sources, 1970), sec. 288.

Hidden in Jesus before the Father

Hidden Life at Nazareth

We usually understand the hidden life of Jesus as refer-
ring to His rather ordinary, daily life for about thirty years at
Nazareth. These years are seen as preparation for the work
and public mission to which Jesus would give Himself for the
last few years of His life. In this understanding, hidden life
means being out of the public eye and out of the mainstream
of activity. There is an obvious truth to this understanding
of the phrase, and it points to a great mystery. When we
appreciate the challenge that awaited Jesus in His public life
and the amount and extent of apostolic work that those last
three years involved, we wonder why He waited so long to
get started. There were so many people whose hearts were
changed and enlivened through Jesus' human encounter with,
His concrete touch upon, their lives. His life and spirit were
so contagious for many. And yet, there were so many others
into whose lives He did not walk and whose hearts He did
not so personally touch—simply because of lack of time
and energy—those inbuilt, human limitations. If He had not
remained hidden for so long, could He not have touched
more and had a more extensive and effective personal

apostolate? There is an amazing mystery here that we must not pass over too lightly.

The mystery is not resolved simply in realizing some particular cultural situation of first-century Palestine. Still, the mystery remains. What is the Father communicating of His view of life through the hidden life of Jesus? Jesus' words at the Last Supper to Phillip give us a glimpse into the deepest identity of this man from Nazareth: "Whoever has seen me has seen the Father" (Jn 14:9). The remark, in a way, explains nothing. But it is a principle of interpretation for everything. It tells us who is revealing, and who and what is being revealed, in every moment and event of this Man's existence.

Hidden in these Nazareth years, then, is a whole vision of life and of true value revelatory of the way our Father and waiting to be communicated to the contemplative heart. And in our contemporary, aggressive, achievement-oriented culture, the heart of the believer needs to taste deeply and regularly the mysterious power and patience of Jesus with His Father in those hidden Nazareth years.

Ultimately, however, Jesus' hidden life remains too superficial and narrow if understood primarily as a preparatory period removed from the public arena of activity. The hidden life of Jesus can and does also describe the life of faith of Jesus in His humanity, and the faith life of each one of us, too, in our following of Him. Thus, quietly but indecisively, the hidden life of Jesus breaks out of the narrow confines of Nazareth. And it will grow to even the deepest and most intimate experience of His Father, in the shockingly public spectacle of the Cross.

Hidden before the Father

Paul's remark in Colossians 3:3, that our true life is a hidden one in God, points to a second understanding of the hidden life: a quality of heart and presence in the very midst of active involvement. In the actions and events of our lives together, we know a great deal about the discrepancy of interpretation, and of experience, too—a discrepancy that occurs both within our own selves and between ourselves and others—depending on whether those actions and events are seen and felt in faith, or are done and discerned apart from faith. But there is a further, dark but beautiful discrepancy that occurs *within* faith: the magnificent distance between what our faith *sees* and *feels* and what our Father knows and is actually accomplishing in and through our lives. Our sensible perception of deeds of faith is always somehow blinded to the hidden fullness of that deed as motivated by faith and love of our God. The fullness of this deed of faith *must* now be hidden to the eyes of faith; it is what the life of faith is all about. But this fullness does register and is known *now* in all its brilliance and simplicity before our Father. One day, our hearts will be expanded in revelation and know clearly and humbly before our Father the fullness of what has been our life of faith.

Now, we live in and work in the hiddenness of faith blinded to the full significance of our deeds and life. We ought not be too preoccupied with this hiddenness. An unduly anxious concern for how worthwhile our lives are and what our lives of faith are really accomplishing often destroys the simple unselfconscious zeal of an apostle. The apostle who loves and serves in faith must learn to act always in peace and in hopeful trust of the fullness of accomplishment before our Father. It may not always be easy for some to avoid such concern about results and to allow Jesus to be our peace in faith and expectation before His and our Father. For Jesus Himself, in His humanity, had to live this life of hidden faith and trust of all that was being accomplished before His Father. This hiddenness of faith kept His heart, and keeps our hearts, transcendently and trustfully open beyond ourselves, to the loving power of a Father who works and surprises us in our zeal. This trustful openness to the Father in every part of our life, an openness called forth by the hidden nature of our faith perception, leads us to a third understanding of Jesus' hidden life.

Hidden Inner Intimacy with the Father

Here, we touch a most profound understanding of Jesus' hidden life, and one that underlies the previous two understandings. For the special quality of heart and the special presence to life described in our second understanding gets its ground and nurture only in a growing interior life of intimacy with the Father. It is this interior life of growing intimacy with the Father that is our third understanding of the hidden life of Jesus. And it brings us to the very heart of the life of faith in each of us.

At this point, let us trace briefly in the Gospels the growth in Jesus of this inner life of intimacy with His Father. I suggest we are talking to the most important theme in the life of Jesus and are at the very heart of the revelation that He is. In our treatment here, we do not pretend to do full justice in length and thoroughness to a theme of such centrality.

We simply mean to suggest a direction that the reader can develop further in prayer and reflection.

In past years, Christians have taken more and more seriously the gradual, very human growth and development of Jesus the man as sent from the Father. This has brought many spiritual blessings and insights in its wake for those carefully contemplating the mysteries of the life of Jesus. Without necessarily being familiar with the subtlety of contemporary professional reflection on the self-consciousness of Jesus, individual believers at prayer have found much light, inspiration, strength, and peace for themselves in the various mysteries of His life. Without in any way denying the divine, eternal sonship of Jesus as revelation sent from the Father, in our reflections here, we will presume and deeply affirm this gradual human growth and developing consciousness of mission and of person—of His entire human existence—and in Him, ours too—as being from, in, and toward the Father.

The Finding in the Temple

A remark of Karl Rahner in his *Spiritual Exercises* points our way here: "If His hidden life was not primarily a religious life, then it is impossible, with the very best will, to find anything really significant about it."[1] In the midst of the ordinariness of His early life in Nazareth, Jesus began to grow in religious experience. As would be true for any young Hebrew boy, Jesus was taught by His mother how to pray and come in touch with the revelation of the Old Testament. We can imagine Jesus at an early stage able to mouth the human words and images of Psalm 139. But it was a special day, finally, when Jesus' own heart was touched in its originality and moved to pray as His own, Psalm 139 to God.

Now, those human words are significative of a sentiment in the heart of this young boy: the beauty of the beginning of a real religious sentiment in His heart. A conscious personal relationship to God begins to grow and mature. Those years in Nazareth hidden from the public eye are specially characterized by this religious growth in the heart of the young man Jesus.

The mystery of the Finding in the Temple pointedly highlights this development in Jesus. The beautiful and very understandable worry and care of Mary and Joseph is met with the mysterious word of Jesus there in the Temple. The verse in Luke 2:49 is translated in many ways, but the core of meaning certainly seems to be: Did you not know I must always be where my Father is? It is a word about the religious experience and identity of Jesus that Mary and Joseph, and Jesus too, had to receive at that moment. This word of truth and identity must have come to them like a two-edged sword that revealed not only Jesus' identity, but also the identity of Mary and Joseph in relationship to Him. Perhaps Mary had to confront for the first time the reality that, although she was His mother, her son did not in some real way belong to her (but, ultimately, the more He is from and for His Father, the more entirely is He hers—and ours). One wonders also whether Jesus Himself did not have to ponder deeply the word of truth and identity that it had been *given* to Him there in His Father's house.

Jesus' prayerful pondering for more than fifteen years would bring a definite religious growth that finally confronted Mary with her son's leaving Nazareth. As His own religious experience and identity continued to grow, a greater interior intimacy with His Father developed. This inner intimacy of real love and trust had now become clear and decisive enough to call Jesus away from Mary and from Nazareth (as Abraham, from Ur; and Moses, from Egypt). It is a beautiful human scene, but surely with a touch of sadness. This woman, who had shared so much of life with her son, on a certain level perhaps not understanding why He must go off to the lonely life of a prophet separate from His whole clan, nevertheless renews her offering of the Annunciation and gives Him over to the world and to the Father. Jesus, knowing now that He must follow the light of His own inner religious intimacy with His Father, sets out very directly and decisively for the Jordan, but only after a tender farewell to His mother. That line of identity—"Did you not know I must always be where my Father is?"—calls Him forth to be where His Father is for Him. It is an identity that will finally bring Him to the Cross. It is the hidden, inner life of intimacy with His Father, then, that calls Jesus out of those hidden years at Nazareth. But we must look to the scene at the Jordan now to appreciate more fully why Jesus leaves Nazareth.

The Jordan Experience

Without any lingering, Jesus goes straightaway from Nazareth to the Jordan to meet with the Baptist. It is precisely a call to the Jordan that has led Him away from all that Nazareth had been to Him.

The Jordan is a scene of sinners of all sorts encountering the Baptist. Within this gathering of sinners, the truth of the Baptist is bluntly calling to repentance and arousing the beginning, graced stirrings of conversion. The whole sinful scene focuses on the starkly prophetic figure of John.

Jesus strides directly into the action and enters it deeply. His words are few, but His behavior and His inner experience reveal the sense of mission and profound religious identity that is growing and moving within Him. Without a word, Jesus gets in line and awaits His turn for baptism—identifying completely with the brotherhood of sin. He takes on the sin of the world. He counters the Baptist's understandable desire to be baptized by Him with words about His need for baptism, that righteousness may be fulfilled.

Then it happens. Whatever the external manifestation precisely was, much more important is the interior experience of Jesus at His Baptism: the power, clarity, and sweetness of His inner religious experience being called by Yahweh: my son, my beloved, my servant. How it must have fired His heart and filled Him with the Spirit! This clear, core identity experience of Jesus results from, brings, and celebrates His profound intimacy with His Father. This core identity experience will be further tested and specified, but it leaves Jesus deeply at prayer in this interior religious experience, even quite oblivious, for the time being, to all that is going on around Him. His prayer could so easily center on Isaiah 41:9-10:

> To say to the prisoners: Come out!
> To those in darkness: Show yourselves!
> Along the roadways they shall find pasture,
> on every barren height shall their pastures be.
> They shall not hunger or thirst;
> nor shall scorching wind or sun strike them;
> For he who pities them leads them
> and guides them beside springs of water.

Propelled by the Spirit of this experience, Jesus leaves the Jordan with an even more intimate inner consciousness of His Father and a sense of His mission as servant for righteousness over sin.

Tempted

With His trust and hope so totally in His Father, Jesus is led by the Spirit into the desert region. The desert with its starkness and simplicity is not a place of superficial experiences. The depth of one's identity is often tested and experienced in the desert. And temptation is always an identity experience, nothing less. Whether in a quiet private area of our hearts or in a dramatically public situation, temptation reveals who we are, who we might mistakenly become, and, finally, who we are *meant* to become. What can often seem so harsh and bleak and austere about the desert can deceptively prevent a person from discovering the beautiful intimacy of the quietly profound, solitary experience of God. But Jesus is not so deceived, for it is the Spirit who leads Him into the vast silence for further confrontation with and specification of His own identity before the Father.

Jesus' experience of the temptations is highlighted when seen in relationship to His Jordan experience. While He is still in immediate touch with His religious experience of being called "my son, my beloved, my servant," in some special way, the three temptations described in the Gospels really challenge the authenticity of that Jordan identity. All the temptations somehow add up to the same thing: if you are the Son of God. Again, whatever the external trappings of this incident were, our chief concern here is the inner experience of Jesus in that growing life of intimacy with His Father.

Is He really son-servant-beloved? Was that Jordan experience illusion? This direct attack on His own inner religious identity must have cost Jesus a great deal of inner reflection and struggle before He could once again choose His Father and, by going with the special experience of being son-servant-beloved, ratify the Jordan experience. The form of presentation of the temptations in the Gospels does not highlight this inner struggle and conflict of Jesus. If misunderstood, the Gospel presentation can make it all seem too easy. But in reality, the issue is tumultuous for the human heart of Jesus. He is asked here to ratify, and thus to embrace, at the level of mission and action, His own relation to the Father.

In each temptation, Jesus is confronted with the alluring attractiveness of Satan's way of being son-servant-beloved. It is a way opposed to the way of His Father. Why not be son-servant-beloved by turning stones to bread? Why not begin the public ministry in this flashy and showy way? In each instance, Jesus must interiorly reject Satan's worldly way of being son-servant-beloved. But this rejection is really a cover for something wonderfully positive: the beautifully intimate inner experience ends there in the desert with Jesus having interpreted His existence and mission in the world at a newly decisive level—all lost in the awesome aloneness of an especially beloved son deeply with His Father, with nothing else mattering, for the moment—and yet, a whole life of love and service definitely, however darkly, contacted in that moment. His hands and His heart and His eyes will continue their human search. And He will need to return here, as He will need to return to other experiences, like Jordan and Tabor, for strength to grapple with the darkness of that human search for His Father in the world.

The desert brings valuable enlightenment and profound growth in Jesus' inner intimacy utterly alone with His Father. And it is the experience of the Father's holiness that creates the imperative of a mission of justice, peace, and forgiving love. This inner life with His Father is creating a whole climate of heart that will continue to grow and to give a warm clarity and decisive direction to His life. Within that climate of heart alone, all future decisions will be made.

The Public Ministry

Jesus comes out of the desert "in the power of the Spirit" (Lk 4:14) and, in Luke's Gospel, goes quite directly to the synagogue in Nazareth where He was raised. In a dramatic scene, Jesus carefully chooses to read a passage of Isaiah:

> The spirit of the Lord GOD is upon me,
> because the LORD has anointed me;
> He has sent me to bring good news to the afflicted,
> to bind up the brokenhearted,
> To proclaim liberty to the captives,
> release to the prisoners,
> To announce a year of favor from the LORD
> and a day of vindication by our God; (Is 61:1-2)

His own brief commentary brings a revelation of His identity. Father Paul Hinnenbusch, in one of his books, says: "The Holy Spirit causes thirst for the Father."[2] That remark can be enlightening here. Jesus comes from that solitude experience in the desert with an all-consuming thirst for His Father, and there is within Him a towering desire to reveal His Father in serving the poor, the captive, the blind, the oppressed, and all who are in need. No wonder the crowds

are amazed at the graciousness of His words! After the profound intimacy of His personal experience alone with His
Father in the desert, His words have an unction and simple
power of conviction that can come no other way. The Spirit
of the Father is so obviously upon Him!

But even here, the angry reaction of the crowd temptingly confronts Him and tries to deter Him from His Father's
way. These moments of temptation and search keep Him in
touch with that inner climate of the heart, that union with
His Father that specifies for Jesus, gradually and increasingly,
His Father's way for being son-servant-beloved. At Caesarea
Philippi, Peter's confession of faith in Jesus' identity is
revealed to be quite superficial and short-visioned when, with
all "good will," he denies Jesus' mission of loving service to
death by the way of the Cross. Jesus rebukes Satan and, once
again, rejects the worldly way by choosing His Father in openness to being with Him, even in the suffering of the Cross.
In the scene of the entry into Jerusalem on Palm Sunday,
the jarring ambiguity between His Father's way of peace and
liberation in Jesus' heart and the superficial, worldly way in
the hearts and voices of the crowd perhaps expresses another
searching confrontation for Jesus.

Another phenomenon of the life of Jesus that is related
to the growth of His hidden life with His Father is His
frequent withdrawal to pray. Just as it is impossible really
to know what Jesus' experiences were like when He was in
that intimate presence of the power and love of His Father
that was His prayer, so it is impossible to deny that He really
needed this special kind of intimate touch with His Father.
His own interior growth and sense of direction and mission
depended very much on these times of prayer. That desert

solitude and intimacy alone with His Father never died but
was continually enkindled. It is important to keep these
experiences of withdrawal in the context and rhythm of His
very active and busy life. These experiences of prayer are
frequently mentioned in the Gospels and are always oriented
to His active life and presence in the world. We are told that
He spent a whole night in prayer with His Father before the
important choice of the Twelve whom He *wanted* as apostles.[3]
In that long night of prayer, as clarity slowly came, these men
were truly *given* to Him by His Father. And at the Last Supper,
He would refer to them in that way in His prayer.[4] The inner
strength and clarity and zeal that came to Jesus from these
times of intimate and intense prayer can be observed in the
quality of His life and activity, although one can only guess
the fullness of what these times meant to Him.

Gethsemane

After the raising of Lazarus, Jesus knows Himself to be
a hunted man because the opposition has now decided to kill
Him and has put out a warrant for His arrest.[5] This burden
in His heart, though it is interrupted in the beauty and direct-
ness of His uninhibited display of love and concern for His
own men in the Cenacle, does give a quiet sense of forebod-
ing to the scene.

Having gone to pray in the olive grove, Jesus is given over
completely to that inner burden. The inner experience of a
sorrow and sadness verging on heartbreak must have regis-
tered on His countenance. Being given an inner revelation
of sin and its horror in a way He never experienced before,
Jesus is all but crushed at the prospect of what is entailed
in being servant for righteousness over sin. The intensity of

the temptation shouts out for support and encouragement. And very little, if any, human support is present. But here, in His lowest moment of tense anguish and loneliness, similar to that of a trapped animal, a gentle strength and a mighty patience is born: "Yet, not as I will, but as you will" (Mt 26:39). The choice of His Father and His way, in an intimacy of trust alone with His Father, reveals here a man with an even deeper awareness now of being son-servant-beloved. The intimacy of that desert moment has been renewed. And as He calls the Apostles to readiness at the end of the agony, there is no longer any sense of being trapped.[6] Rather, there stands and strides forward the Son, at one with His Father in obedience and confidence to the end.

Beloved and Trusting on the Cross

This intimacy is especially hidden in Jesus through His Passion, except for that patience and that power in silence that can come from nothing but His inner union with his Father. But it is on the Cross that this hidden inner life of Jesus reaches its climax in a final trusting surrender—its climax of hiddenness and its climax as a life lived in God.

The jeers and taunts hurled at Jesus on the Cross contain the full temptation of worldly unbelief. Once again, the point is the same: "If you are the Son of God, come down from the cross" (Mt. 27:40). Jesus must choose again to be son-servant-beloved according to His Father's way of love. The situation, in its external appearance, is the height of absurdity. A promising young Hebrew man at the height of His power and of His attractiveness for His people is being asked to disengage from life—the utter foolishness of the Cross. Significance and redemption are found, here above all, only

in the inner life of Jesus with His Father on the Cross. The
Death on the Cross gives final definitive and everlasting form
to Jesus' intimate, loving trust of His Father. This disengagement from life by Jesus is His greatest act of trust in His
Father. And it brings for Him, and for everybody, the fullness
of life. Those words in the temple—"Did you not know that
I must be in my Father's house?" (Lk 2:49)—they have led to
this. And Mary hears those words differently here on Calvary.
She has treasured them in her heart for very long.

Jesus' words from the Cross are almost responses to the
taunts hurled at the Cross. But then, He cries out in the inner
bleakness of forsaken aloneness: "My God, my God, why
have you forsaken me?" (Mt 27:46) There is a great mystery
here. But He seems to be doing more than simply reciting
Psalm 22. Somehow, His inner experience, just for a moment,
finds Him utterly bereft of His Father. Sin now has had its
way fully, and somehow Jesus seems and feels Himself to
be without His Father. And this is the final gift. For this is a
man who loved His human life and the exploration of His
talents. And the Cross is the destruction of all that. Further,
this is not only a man, but a Jewish man. And now He hangs
repudiated and driven from His people. But if you go to the
core of Him the primary, growing definitive identity and consciousness of Jesus is to be His Father's son, His servant, His
beloved. And here on the Cross—for a moment—in the final
foolishness of love, the felt experience of this, too, is given
over: "My God, my God, why have you forsaken me?"

But even in that moment, Jesus does not really lose hope
and trust. And so, sin's sway over the world is ended and
broken by the loving trust of the Obedient One. And, perhaps, out of the bleak barrenness of that dark moment, there

sounds in the heart of Jesus the loving call of His Father in the words of the Song of Songs:

> My lover speaks and says to me,
> "Arise, my friend, my beautiful one,
> and come!
> For see, the winter is past,
> the rains are over and gone.
> The flowers appear on the earth,
> the time of pruning the vines has come,
> and the song of the turtledove is heard in our land.
> The fig tree puts forth its figs,
> and the vines, in bloom, give forth fragrance.
> Arise, my friend, my beautiful one,
> and come!
> My dove in the clefts of the rock,
> in the secret recesses of the cliff,
> Let me see your face,
> let me hear your voice,
> For your voice is sweet,
> and your face is lovely." (Sg 2:10-14)

"Arise, my friend, my beautiful one, and come!" It is the Father, calling Jesus home now, in hidden intimacy that defies description, where "He will wipe every tear from their eyes, and there shall be no more death or mourning, wailing or pain" (Rev 21:4)—not only for Him but for the total world of all His brothers and sisters who are here, on the Cross, taken up into His own final loveliness.

In this way, the light and joy of Resurrection is somehow present and beginning there, in the dying. For a man to die in that way is to be assured of new risen life. And so, Jesus' last words on the Cross are a response to His Father out of the profound, powerful, inner intimacy of His heart: "Father, my Father, into your hands I give over my heart." It is the Son who speaks, obediently and intimately, beloved servant to the end!

Our Life of Faith

Let us now turn to some reflections on our own lives in the light of Jesus' hidden life with His Father. We are called to share and live in some similar way this inner life. It is Jesus as Risen Lord who makes possible this inner life our Father desires to share with each of us: "Everything has been entrusted to me by my Father; and no one knows who the Son is except the Father, and who the Father is except the Son and those to whom the Son chooses to reveal him" (Lk 10:22). It is overwhelming but true that this is precisely what the life of faith is all about. Faith is not simply a matter of external actions, or words, or of certain thoughts. All these, without the inner intimacy of love and trust of the Father, turn faith into an empty shell. Thus, faith requires a continual conversion of our sin-stained affectivity into the true, living affectivity of the Risen Jesus who is now entirely at one with His Father in the desire to console all of us by sharing with us their inner life together. It is this inner hidden life of faith that always distinguishes the true believer from the secular humanist.

The climate of the heart that this hidden life creates should be the atmosphere within which all our decisions become clear and out of which all our actions spring. In this way, all our slightest interior movements are discerned in consonance with the peace and intimacy of our Father in our hearts. The inner affective experience of peace in our Father becomes thus the birth place of an indomitable zeal.

This zeal and desire to do great things for God is often expressed quietly and humbly in the eager readiness to do the next deed as discovered through intimacy with the Father in Jesus. So this hidden life of intimacy is not simply a matter of prayer and of inner religious experience that is oblivious of our real world in it struggle for redemption and justice and peace. This hidden life inevitably takes expression in a special, vital quality of presence in our world and in the midst of the most active situations. It is a presence characterized in faith by peace, gentleness, joy, humble gratitude, and decisive zeal. This quality of presence in the world requires careful contemplation of the mysteries of Jesus' life, a contemplation which brings an inner harmony with His own hidden life of intimate trust and love of His Father. This kind of presence in any situation of our troubled world is rarely easy, since it is often so counter-cultural. But it is always decisive in faith for the kingdom of our Father in Christ.

Finally, this inner hidden life of faith enriches our appreciation of the Trinity of God, and it reveals the Trinitarian dimension in even the most ordinary of our experiences. We can understand the Holy Spirit as all that inner richness of intimacy and love that is between Son and Father. And Jesus returned to His Father so we could live in His Spirit and continually grow in that hidden inner life of intimacy with His Father. He desires this, that the world may come to believe in Him who is our Father and in his only Son, Jesus Christ who, together, now send us the Spirit:

> that he may grant you in accord with the riches of his glory to be strengthened with power through his Spirit

in the inner self, and that Christ may dwell in your hearts through faith" (Eph 3:16-17).

NOTES

1.   Karl Rahner, S.J., *Spiritual Exercises* (New York: Herder and Herder, 1965), 157.

2.   Paul Hinnenbusch, O.P., *Prayer: The Search for Authenticity* (New York: Sheed and Ward, 1969), 22.

3.   See Luke 6:12-13.

4.   See John 13:1.

5.   See Luke 11:53-54.

6.   See Mark 14:41-42.

COMPARISON AND COMPETITION STIFLING SPIRITUAL INTIMACY

Human persons are so naturally social that comparison leading to competition will always be rife in human culture. It is so endemic to our human condition that no one of us fully avoids it. And as we have long since learned from our study of psychology, such matters are not simply stamped out or repressed. They are dealt with. Comparison and competition challenge our very identity. Either they almost destroy us, or they build us up in a humble confidence of being loved and cared for, come what may. Comparison and competition, properly dealt with in faith, can root us deeply in God and form us into a community for service.

A Desire to Be Famous, to Be Someone Special

Comparison is closely related to the desire to be known and loved, to be recognized and to be famous, a desire that is so deep in the human psyche. Neither right nor wrong in itself, this desire is just part of who we are and immediately puts us in relation to others. These relations always involve looking at one another—which, if not always, is often to compare. And such comparison frequently has a competitive edge to it. To the extent that it does, it is corrupting of healthy human relationships. We manage this desire for fame variously: sometimes, by outright denial; sometimes, through another kind of defense, by an egotism that is obnoxious to everybody, even ourselves. Another alternative, however, for basically resolving this desire for love and recognition is honestly acknowledging it and actively integrating it within the daily complexity of all the relationships of our lives. Therefore, it is the way in which we recognize and deal with the desire that makes all the difference.

The affective register of comparison and competition in each of us is envy and jealousy. These frequent affections of our hearts, when viewed in faith, are part of the sinful human condition, the remedy of which is a Father's forgiving love in Jesus, available daily to integrate and identify us. Although their effect may be very subtle, the natural dynamic of envy and jealousy creates distance and works an insidious divisiveness into relationships.

Religious communities also have their own patterns of these affections. Petty envy and jealousies can continuously undercut unity among members. The competition in a community can be very keen for those apostolic assignments that have a salary attached or that bring public prestige. Not many want to serve in the community infirmary!

A brief look at our culture today reveals how timely and important our topic is from another perspective. The Madison Avenues of capitalism thrive on comparison and competition. Underneath the cultivated homey or humorous veneer of advertising is a deadly serious business that strives to create slavish dependency. Each fall an entire issue of the *New York Times Magazine* seductively dictates every detail of fashion. In this "future shock" world of the disposable, who dares break through the fashion barrier and actually wear clothes till they wear out?

Advertising's pitch hits us where we are often most susceptible. We are told that we must be attractive or beautiful if we want to matter—these are the subliminal motives that fuel so much advertising. These are fundamental issues, around which all of us have strong feelings and desires. Having studied the human animal closely, Madison Avenue knows which nerve to touch in order to achieve the desired effect. In this way, our value and identity are at issue every time we watch television or read a magazine. In our moments of maturity and peaceful self-possession, we ridicule this process. But how often the "hidden persuader" successfully works his insidious control and traps us into a pathetic loss of freedom. Even more tragic is the desolate frustration of those people who are hypnotized into believing that their beauty and dignity really do reside in a three-piece suit or a brand of perfume, and yet who must live with the shattering knowledge that they will never be able to afford such things.

A Self-Centered Experience

I have been speaking of the relational character of comparison and competition. However, despite their outward reference, they are very self-centered concerns. People who lack the confidence of a good, realistic self-image are especially prone to comparison and competition. So many people, behind a superficially confident exterior, reveal a great inner fragility and are in need of excessive affirmation. For such people, identity itself is at issue in most situations of their lives. Underneath all other concerns lies the major one in which an appalling amount of psychic energy and anxiety is invested: "How am I doing?" The question of self-worth dominates all interaction with other people. The issue of "How am I doing?" leads very naturally to comparative and competitive glances at our brothers and sisters. If I am doing at least as well as they are, I am safe. If I am doing better than they are, so much the better for me.

The search for this kind of self-image, and the excessive need for affirmation that follows from it, unconsciously sets off various self-centered dynamics in us. First of all, poor self-image can serve as a self-fulfilling prophecy. Because we feel so down on ourselves as unlovable and unvaluable, we will use every event of life to prove to ourselves and others how correct is our judgment of our low self-worth. A false humility can either refuse to be complemented or unjustifiably take the blame for everything.

In another, paradoxical way, an arrogant, self-righteous superiority defends us against having to face our true lack of self-worth. This superior attitude can infiltrate into everything, leading us into working overtime to prove how competent and confident we are. Now, everybody else feels put down in relation to us. The pharisee praying in the temple, despite his genuine generosity, seems to be an example of this type of person.[1]

There is a third way in which those with a weak self-concept may manipulate approval and affirmation in every situation. It is pathetic but understandable to hear someone "objectively" read approval and congratulation of self into a situation where the person's faulty performance is actually resulting in a lack of approval and satisfaction.

As indicated, for people of fragile self-concept, these dynamics keep the self very central in the heart's stage. But let us be realistic. Self-worth is a problem for all of us and is so much a part of the human condition that it hovers in the wings of the stage of every human heart. But this concern need not be center stage. And it will not be, if *life* is center stage. And life will be center stage to the extent that I am at home with myself and not in doubt about my own radical self-worth.

Change in the Apostles

It is instructive for our topic to look at the Apostles in the Scriptures. Throughout the Gospels, we find them very humanly concerned about how they are doing and searching, often in very competitive comparisons, for the answer. More than once, when Jesus asks them what they have been talking about, their embarrassed response indicates their preoccupation with who from among them will be greatest or first in the kingdom. When it seems that James and John may receive special honor, the jealous, angry wrangling begins.[2] Jesus speaks to the issue very directly by describing his revolution of love, service, and power. But the Apostles do not understand yet. Even at the Last Supper, the insidious concern of "How am I doing?" is still present.[3] The Apostles are like so many of us—unfree, often drained of enthusiasm and energy because of that unanswered central question: "How am I doing?" As long as this question is unanswered, we look to others in a gaze of competitive comparison, and we cannot really see all that is there.

But in the Acts of the Apostles, at least after Pentecost, the scene is changed. The Apostles' hearts have been refocused. We find not a moment of worry and wasted energy on "how they are doing." That question seems basically inoperative now.[4] The whole energy of their hearts is focused on "What is the Spirit moving us to do so that the Lord Jesus may be more widely known and served and so that more brothers and sisters may know His Father's forgiving and freeing love?" This becomes the life of their consciousness now. The gaze of their hearts is extroverted in the realization of the Father's raising Jesus to new life. The question of self-worth has been answered, and so, without the interference of competitive comparison, they see their brothers and sisters in a wholly new light. Now, they understand Jesus' words and example about humble service. Confidently, they live a new humility.[5] Louis Evely's words on humility seem very apposite here: " . . . Humility is a consequence of love . . . It is to be not self-satisfied, it is not to worry about one's glory . . . It is to put one's delight so much in another that one no longer thinks of oneself."[6]

Identified in the Cross

This development of identity and humility, the foundation for any true apostleship, brings an integration in faith and makes possible a whole different presence on the part of the apostle. And it is a development that is rooted in, and the product of, Jesus' own experience of His Father's fidelity in and through His Death on the Cross. Furthermore, sharing this experience of Jesus on the Cross is to receive an identity forged in forgiveness.[7]

All through His life, Jesus gradually rooted His identity in Yahweh as the one whom He called "my Father." Day by day, He learned to live out of that identity. A life-long process of temptation tested His identity. The issue was always the same: His Father's love and care, come what may.[8]

Soon after Caesarea Philippi and Peter's limited profession
of faith, Jesus moves from a fairly successful Galilean ministry to a Jerusalem ministry that is not so promising.[9] And
this juncture, which is often considered a turning point and
which begins the disengagement from the apparent success
in Galilee, marks the first prediction of the Passion and is
shortly followed by the clarification of the Transfiguration,
where, as in the Baptism, He is specially claimed as Son by
a delighted Father. The intimate, trusting abandonment to
His Father that this whole period manifests is highlighted by
the certainty and force of His rebuke to Peter: "'Get behind
me, Satan! . . . You are thinking not as God does, but as
human beings do'" (Mt 16:13-23). When the opposition goes
public and the decision for Jesus' Death is publicized,[10] He
withdraws to Ephraim bordering the desert, where, long ago,
in the face of special temptation, His Father's attractive love
had previously identified Him.[11] And from the midst of that
renewed intimacy with his Father comes the decision to go
for His Passover—perhaps, the most courageous choice of
His Father thus far.

The choice of Jesus' Father in the face of death was not
the obviously right one from every angle. From many sides, it
must have seemed absurd: almost at the height of His power
of influence for good, not an old man ready to die, with so
many more people still to know His Father's kingdom, why
not avoid this Jerusalem way and escape to another way?
His Father's loving and firm call hearkening in His heart
transcends the absurdity, and He goes with and to His Father
in Jerusalem. And then, the consequent abandonment in
Gethsemane further places all hope and the future itself in
the Father, and brings an intimate and sturdy confidence to

go on. Finally, in that ultimate experience of His ignominious death, when all hope seems gone and even the felt experience of His Father is removed, He dies. He dies in trust and hope, only *apparently* all alone. For in the deepest center of this dying, the One who had always been the simple and fully Obedient Son finds a Father's blessing and fidelity expressed in the Resurrection, an absolutely indestructible presence and union till the end of time—and beyond. All reality has been changed here. The human bondage and limits of sin and death have been smashed, and life is much fuller and more expansively abundant than ever before.[12]

This experience of a Father's identifying His Son in fidelity with new life in the depths of dying is meant for all of us. In this ultimate moment of death, abandoned and stripped of everything, Jesus discovers a Father's fidelity and presence. In this ultimate situation, when all seems lost, if a Father's life and love are present, then no situation can ever be ultimately and truly hopeless. Even the sinner knows a Father's presence beseeching repentance. As we contemplatively share this crucial experience of Jesus, something which begins to happen at our Baptism,[13] we are identified by our faithfully loving Father in the beautifully trusting Spirit of His Jesus. This experience of new life in the dying of Jesus reveals a love and forgiveness for us that can never be surpassed—a belief in us and an affirmation of our beauty and value beyond anything this world can offer.

This unique, all-alone experience of God in Jesus makes a great spiritual intimacy available in faith. Surely, this is not a once-in-a-lifetime experience. Just the opposite. This identity experience of God in Jesus continues to grow, is supposed to grow, all through our lives. It is an ongoing experience aimed at rooting and directing our whole life. It is a monotheistic experience, an experience of God, a God whose love and life far surpass any other goodness of this world. This experience of the one and only true God, this pastoral and not just doctrinal monotheism, strips our idol-worshipping hearts and thereby establishes and keeps all remaining reality in proper perspective—including all the apostolic realities that need our present love and service. Knowing this one, true God *beyond* all else makes us capable of His presence *in* all else and brings an intimacy in faith, an experience of being loved and valued, absolutely so, beyond any comparison and all competition. Monotheism, then, is no arbitrary cultural experience of the Hebrew people, but a revealer of the depth and expansiveness of the human heart in every age. As such, it undermines every competitive comparison, even as it calls forth confident servant love.

Envy and Jealousy Transformed

Even for someone identified before the Cross of Jesus, envy and jealousy do not disappear. Certain external situations continue to provoke the inner affective reaction of envy and jealousy. But now, we can be quicker to recognize what is happening within us; and, therefore, we are able to deal with it more decisively, preventing it from dominating our external actions and presence among other people. Our own feelings of being overlooked and almost rejected because someone else is in the limelight of success and public honor can hardly be avoided at certain times. This feeling of being all alone and cut off from others, which is what envy and jealousy do to us, need not provoke its own behavior. We are not trapped in the envy and jealousy; but within them, we can hear a call to something else. The mature, self-possessed person, without resorting to any unhealthy repression, recognizes what is happening and does not fear its alone-ness. Rather, in the alone-ness, an opportunity lies to renew that identity in spiritual intimacy alone before God in Jesus, where love and acceptance can never falter.

In this way, envious and jealous feelings can lead us quietly, without anyone else's realizing it, to be alone with our loving Father who sees and rewards all that is done in secret.[14] This secret renewal of self makes possible sharing in the celebration of another's success, peacefully and genuinely, beyond any personal need now to be affirmed and publicly acclaimed. For someone not identified in Jesus' Cross, the envious, jealous, lonely seclusion gets acted out in any number of ways; and the spiritual intimacy, offered in secret, is not received. On the other hand, the one maturely identified in God still enjoys and feels good about public acclaim and affirmation, but has no special need of it. It is interesting to notice that, in the very extensive and thorough *Study of Readiness for Ministry* by the Association of Theological Schools, the top quality desired in a good pastoral minister is "service without regard for acclaim . . . without concern for public recognition."[15] This is a minister whose behavior and service is not ruled by comparison and competition.

Community and Service Beyond Competitive Comparison

The identity wrought by knowing, in the hiddenness of the crucified Jesus, the secret reward of a faithful Father, while it is often renewed in the aloneness of envious and jealous feelings, certainly does not keep us withdrawn and unconcerned with the world. Rather, it powerfully impels us in two very extroverted directions.

First, this identity makes possible a sharing in community that is centered on God, beyond any need for comparison or for a confidence derived from a sense of superiority. People identified by God in Christ come to one another out of the spiritual intimacy with the Father that is born in the radical solitude of their own hearts. They are capable of building one another up in love by allowing God's grace to call forth the best from each, without any competitive divisiveness. In a religious community, the vows have their own specific way of expressing our radical trust in a Father's love—a trust and love ultimately shown forth in Jesus' dying. In the shared experience of obedience, the abandonment of "being sent" unites all the members and creates essential equality among all the works of the community, regardless of financial remuneration and public acclaim. In this way alone, the understandable but divisive competition for apostolic assignments can be dispelled, and in Christ, the ground for each competition disappears.

Second, such an identity in Christ Jesus crucified impels us to concern and service for all in our world. God's vision of justice for our world, as displayed in the dying and rising of the Lord, becomes the priority of our hearts—and of our deeds. With our identity focused and concentrated, we are driven by our Father's love to serve others. Awareness of our Father's loving acceptance of us, far beyond anything of our own deserving, inspires a special quality of loving service. As an expression of our gratitude, our service is not contained by the ordinary limits of comfort, convenience, and enjoyment, but rather is characterized by the attitude of "nothing

is too much." Identified and confident of our value, we are
capable of service in the face of insult and humiliation, without the need for self-affirmation and self-esteem from others
in all we do. More and more, situations in our unjust and
secularistic world are calling for men and women who can
serve in just this way.

Competition, at once, causes, signals, and results from
stifled spiritual intimacy, which is to lose the enormous apostolic power of humble, generous, extroverted existence. Life
is given and lived out of a radical awareness of our Father's
faithful and forgiving acceptance of us in the trusting Spirit
of His Jesus. Such acceptance brings a spiritual intimacy in
faith that is unique to each and every one of us. It is our
personal mystery, friendly and collaborative, but wholly
beyond compare.

NOTES

1. See Luke 18:9-14.
2. See Matthew 20:20-28.
3. See Luke 22:24-27.
4. I am not concerned with the ordinary foibles of human life and personality. I am thinking of the substantive reorientations and redemptive extroversion that one finds in the book of the Acts.
5. I first heard this idea of the growth in the Apostles presented in a retreat conference by John Staudenmaier, S.J.
6. Louis Evely, *A Religion for Our Time* (New York: Herder and Herder, 1968), 57.
7. See the essay "Forgiveness" in this book.
8. See the essay "Hidden in Jesus before the Father" in this book.
9. I am relying here, of course, on synoptic perspective.
10. See John 11:53-57.
11. See Matthew 4:1-11.
12. See John 10:10.
13. See Romans 6:1-8.
14. See Matthew 6:4-6.
15. *Readiness for Ministry*, Vol. 1, Criteria (Vandalia, Ohio: The Association of Theological Schools in the United States and Canada, 1976), 6.

FORGIVENESS

All our lives, we are in search of our true selves. Many people's search for self-value and self-worth reaches a frenetic pitch. Our culture has provided some new and exciting avenues for the search though they are known already to be dead-ends. Saint Augustine would remind us that true knowledge of self is impossible without the intimate knowledge of Our Father and Creator. If it is His creative loving gaze on us that breathes life into us from moment to moment, then really to know Him is to discover ourselves.

We receive ourselves as gifts from others, but most especially from Another, Our Father and Creator. And so, our true worth so clearly is in being loved and in loving. But this discovery of our genuine dignity essentially involves the experience of being forgiven. Jesus' words to the woman at Simon's dinner express it well: "So I tell you, her many sins have been forgiven; hence, she has shown great love. But the one to whom little is forgiven, loves little" (Lk 7:47). The experience of forgiveness reveals and integrates all our energies for living and loving in all situations as sons and daughters of a loving Father.

There is often a great anxiety at the prospect of facing one's self. However, the ultimate sadness is to live life in darkness—without the enlightenment of *knowing* the mystery of ourselves mirrored in God's great hopes and dreams for each one of us. Any humiliation and worry and fear is worth that ultimate discovery!

Our Need to Be Helped

The journey to self-identity commences with the realization of our need to be helped. Our real self-worth and identity is given only in forgiveness; it is never self-fabricated. The first real step toward self-identity is allowing God to reveal our sinfulness. This is never easy, especially not today. Many people are anguishing over questions such as these: Is there such a thing as sin? Does not the old notion of sin lead to neurotic guilt complexes and self-hatred? And what does all this imply about a loving God? In a world so filled with evil who, if anybody, is to be blamed for the sin?

The Church is experiencing the inevitable confusion of a transitional growth in her understanding of the mystery of sinfulness, which obviously is affecting many other things, such as the use of the Sacrament of Penance. However, this confusion is most urgent in its effect on our deepest Christian self-identity through forgiveness. One can see much evidence today of this basic identity confusion in the Church and in the world.

Our sinfulness is not something we can become aware of all by ourselves if we put our mind to recalling past failures. Too often, this is where we look for our own sense of sin. God, however, must *reveal* to us our sinfulness. There is no other way to come to it. In the light of His love for us, our sinfulness is revealed. Many times, when we pray carefully about our Father's uniquely personal love for us, a kind of uneasiness begins to stir in our hearts. This can be the beginning of the revelation of sinfulness. The more intimately and personally aware we become of His love for us, the more our sense of sinfulness is revealed. Since the mystery of sinfulness must be revealed by God, we should pray for it if we truly desire to know ourselves.

In this sense, we can speak of the *grace* of sinfulness. To be more and more aware of the mystery of sinfulness in our hearts is a grace given only by God. Such an awareness is not received through an introspective moralistic examination of conscience. We need to be more reverently and humbly aware of the intimacy and depth of detail of His love for us rather than to stir up our own guilt-laden anxiety over past failures. If we really could know how much God loves us, we would be intensely aware in sorrow of our sinfulness! To stand openly in the light of His love will touch off in our hearts the shame, embarrassment, and sorrow of a sinner.

There is an unhealthy guilt and anxiety that is not relational; it does not draw us beyond ourselves. It simmers in our hearts and corrodes our peace. The grace of sinfulness is quite otherwise. We can make one another feel guilty but not sinful. Only a relation beyond ourselves to God's goodness and holiness reveals our sinfulness. A deficient sense of sin usually speaks of a deficient or immature relationship with God.

For some people, sin is a juridical matter—serious in itself and consciously posited in a voluntary action. Within this minimal conception of sin, it is difficult for many to experience the Spirit of God accusing them of sin as in 1 John 1:10: "If we say, 'We have not sinned,' we make him a liar, and his word is not in us." A growth in faith experience brings us to a more refined sense of sinfulness beyond the juridical concept of actions posited.

Paul says in Romans 14:23: "Whatever is not from faith is sin." Here, we have a much more mature sense of sinfulness recognized in direct proportion to the extent and depth of our faith experience. To be juridical and childishly automatic about faith is to maintain a minimal sense of sinfulness. To have the blindness of our unbelief pierced by the light of faith brings concomitantly a sense of our sinful past. This sense of sinfulness is not as much dependent on consciously posited actions as on the objective fact—*then* not consciously recognized but now enlightened in faith—of a past life of ignorance of and blindness to the reality of God. A grown person *now* intimately aware of his loving Father can be deeply sorrowful for repeated rebellious refusals in his teens to worship the Father who was *then* so loving and gracious to him. No wonder the saints who love so deeply in joyful and grateful faith know themselves to be so deeply sinful. This same vision of the relationship between sinfulness and faith can face the confessor with the danger of interpreting what he hears in the light of his own weak faith and erroneously trying to inform the deeply gifted penitent that what was confessed is not really a sin. A live sense of sinfulness and an intimate awareness of a loving Father gifting us in all are inseparable!

A passing and temporary trial of slight scrupulosity often accompanies this growing refinement of a sense of sinfulness. We must be careful to interpret this interior movement as a good healthy sign. We are not, here, talking of a pathological emotional disorder. A person's conscience is simply

catching up with his faith! This happened in the conversion
of Saint Ignatius Loyola and of many other saints.

A Dynamic Reality

Our awareness of sinfulness grows gradually. What
might first register as guilt will soon grow to shame and sorrow as sin is situated within the context of a personal love
relationship with our loving Father gifting us in everything.
To appreciate sin from God's viewpoint is to bring shame,
embarrassment, and confusion into our heart. This is neither
a nice nor pleasant experience but a deeply Christian one and
it verges on the discovery of gratitude in forgiveness. It is a
consolation and a grace. Because it is a true experience of
God, it is, therefore, compatible with a deep peace and even a
quiet joy.

Self-hatred is something very different from awareness of
sinfulness and can be a real interference to the genuine grace
of sinfulness manifesting itself in shame, embarrassment,
and confusion in the awareness given us of our sinfulness by
a Father who continues *right now* to love and gift us. To face
our sinfulness and ingratitude outside of the presence of our
loving Father is always destructive and not renewing. It is
precisely the tangible evidence of His continuing love *here and
now* that brings the shame and embarrassment and confusion.
His mercy has always been there; in fact, our sin stands out
precisely in that contrast. There can be a subtle temptation,
however, to avoid the shame and sorrow of our sins by con-
centrating too simply, and yet superficially, on God's love for
us. To give real body and depth of our song of gratitude in
forgiveness, we must see the mystery of *what* is forgiven. Only
in appreciating the costliness of the forgiveness can we avoid

too superficial a sense of our dignity as sons and daughters sharing God's life and Spirit.

It is not enough to see sin as harming ourselves or other people. We need to have revealed to us the disappointment that sin is to God. We need to see our own ungrateful and insensitive response in terms of our gracious Father, so disappointed, puzzling over the mystery of the "sour grapes" in Isaiah 5:4, "What more could be done for my vineyard that I did not do? Why, when I waited for the crop of grapes, did it yield rotten grapes?" This can be a powerful moment in the dynamic of the grace of sinfulness; a moment, too, that makes possible a deeper experience of the absolute gratuity of God's forgiveness.

Unless we come, in grace, to see that our sinfulness in its blindness, insensitivity, and rebellion (however polite or civilized!) does not deserve forgiveness, we superficialize our Father's loving forgiveness of us. Without the frightening awareness that our sins really deserve to be punished and even to have us rubbed out of existence, we take very much for granted our Father's forgiveness and turn it into a cheap commodity. We lose the sense of the precious, and our life is deprived of deep reverence. "If you, Lord, keep account of sins, Lord, who can stand? But with you is forgiveness and so you are revered" (Ps 130:3-4). This realization of our sin's relationship to our loving Father is a grace. This realization brings the basic experience of being ashamed and embarrassed in the presence of God, which does not prevent the full joy, surprise, and gratitude of knowing the gratuitousness of His forgiveness of us. It is, rather, the awareness of living on "borrowed time," as that is lovingly given by a Father whose fidelity is beyond question. But it is *borrowed* time! Borrowed time, nevertheless, that in this victoriously given Father's love becomes *our* time, in the raising of His crucified Christ.

Another moment in the dynamic that is the grace of sinfulness leading to forgiveness can be one of real fright. It is what Paul speaks of in Romans 7:24: "Miserable one that I am! Who will deliver me from this mortal body?" This can be a moment of sobering realization of how trapped we are. To fixate on this moment is to despair. The grace of this moment, which may last quite a while, is to call forth in deep, joyful gratitude the realization in faith of the Father's forgiveness, Who is Jesus on the Cross. It brings the intimate love-experience of Jesus, which is salvation and which reorients a person's whole life. "Thanks be to God through Jesus Christ our Lord" (Rom 7:25).

As the moments of shame, embarrassment, and confusion pass through a frightening fear and grow to deep sorrow in the presence of our Father whose love is constant, in the very depths of our sense of sinfulness, there comes the strong and joyful gratitude of a helplessly trapped sinner suddenly and freely forgiven—for no reason but the mystery of a Father's love expressed in forgiveness. The joy, peace, and gratitude of forgiveness do not replace the sinfulness; rather, they complement and transform it. One has seen his selfish sinfulness too deeply ever to forget that aspect of self-knowledge. So that even in the joy and gratitude, there is always and easily an element of sorrow. In this life, we never step beyond the awareness of our sinfulness.

Renewal through Humiliation

In tracing the development of the various moments in the grace of our sinfulness as that happens in us, we are demonstrating that forgiveness itself is a process in us. It is the process of conversion into and discovery of our true selves. Far from happening instantaneously, this is a lifetime growth process, though there usually are periods of greater intensity. In all of us, there are areas of our heart that need to experience the Father's forgiveness Who is Jesus. In these areas of our heart, we are still not truly free; we are not truly ourselves because Jesus is not Lord for us there yet.

In these unredeemed parts of our heart, we have not humbly acknowledged sin. Our proud independence often prevents the humiliation inevitable for new life in forgiveness. Roustang says in *Growth in the Spirit*, "If in the least particle of ourselves we think we are just through our own efforts, into this tiny particle Christ cannot bring the gratuitousness of his salvation."[1] Forgiveness can take effect only through the humiliating acknowledgement of sinfulness. It is the hopeful cry for help in our need that calls forth our Father's forgiveness. "A bruised weed he will not break, and a dimly burning wick he will not quench" (Is 42:3). It is much easier to talk about humility than to feel the hurting sting and shame of humiliation before our loving Father. However, to avoid or rationalize away or go light on this shameful humiliation is to lighten the experience of new life through His forgiveness. Forgiveness can happen in no other way. And yet, our sinful selves will always squirm before this searing humiliation. Forgiveness is always a Paschal experience—something must die in shame if new life is to be given in love.

Often in an ordinary use of the Sacrament of Penance, the humiliation can be as simple and yet elusive as the admission that I have not yet allowed myself to be cleansed of those same small acts of ingratitude to God. It humiliates us to admit that honestly before our Father in the presence of a human minister of the Church. To avoid this personal shame before our Father is to avoid the very depths of our understanding of sin and until we come to appreciate the humiliation involved in forgiveness, we will not appreciate the new view of the Sacrament of Penance as not just for removing serious sins but much more—for continuing spiritual progress in God's forgiveness.

Life as Thanksgiving

Realized forgiveness turns life itself into thanksgiving and wonder. The dynamic of the grace of sinfulness always concludes in gratitude. Our Father is with us daily to convert us from sinfulness to free and joyful gratitude through the mysterious power of His forgiveness in our humiliated powerlessness. Gratitude is the truest identity of the Christian believer. But only scars of shame and humiliation can remind us reverently of its precious quality. Often, fear of the pain of confronting the revelation of our humiliating sinfulness impedes a more invigorating experience of forgiveness and, thus, keeps us only on the surface of thanksgiving. We do not find our real selves in peace and in joy and in Christ who is the Father's forgiveness.

The gratitude in our forgiveness motivates our every action. To be a grateful person in everything is the clearest sign of a believer. "And be thankful. . . . And whatever you do, in word or in deed, do everything in the name of the Lord

Jesus, giving thanks to God the Father through him" (Col 3:15,17).

This thanksgiving will daily take expression joyously in humble, loving service without any pretense or delusion of selfish grandeur and power. The sorrow, now turned into joy, has not been completely forgotten. Gentleness and reverence are close at hand because the grateful person finds the forgiving hand of the Father in everything. "Your kindness should be known to all. The Lord is near" (Phil 4:5). The grateful heart is constantly growing in wonder and awe, giving sight to eyes to see what and who really is present in all.

Ministry of Reconciliation Among Men

We live today in a world so much in need of forgiveness. Hearts shamed and embarrassed in the uneasy need for forgiveness and healing often cover up with a thin politeness or a facade of smug self-sufficiency. They cry out, however, for the experience of gratitude. In religious life, as we are led into a new age, one of our greatest needs is to forgive one another. The daily newspaper reveals on all levels of our society and on the international scene the painful evidence of the need for forgiveness and for healing. The ministry of reconciliation is so much in demand today. How much the embarrassed smugness and the frightened sadness want to smile in healed thanksgiving! But we must appreciate the depth of this demand on us all. Without a gratitude daily deepening in our experience of our Father's free forgiveness of us, our own involvement in a ministry of reconciliation cannot succeed. He is always the initiative and the example of how true forgiveness happens. "Be merciful just as [also] your Father is merciful. 'Stop judging and you will not be judged.

Stop condemning and you will not be condemned. Forgive
and you will be forgiven"' (Lk. 6:36-37). The joyous good
news of a Father's gracious forgiveness can only be known as
it is lived and shared by His sons and daughters in our world.
Saint Paul is beautiful and clear in 2 Cor. 5:17-12:

> So whoever is in Christ is a new creation: the old things
> have passed away; behold, new things have come.
> And all this is from God, who has reconciled us to
> himself through Christ and given us the ministry of
> reconciliation, namely, God was reconciling the world to
> himself in Christ, not counting their trespasses against
> them and entrusting to us the message of reconciliation.
> So we are ambassadors for Christ, as if God were
> appealing through us. We implore you on behalf of
> Christ, be reconciled to God. For our sake he made him
> to be sin who did not know sin, so that we might become
> the righteousness of God in him.

Reconciliation among men requires far more than a
grasp of the dynamics of interpersonal relationships and the
demands of justice and the protocol of equity.

True self-worth and identity is never found through the
power and force of self-assertion. It is never self-fabricated!
It must be gratefully received in the experience of a Father's
forgiveness. "So I tell you, her many sins have been forgiven;
hence, she has shown great love. But the one to whom little is
forgiven, loves little" (Lk 7:47).

NOTES

1.   Francois Roustang, *Growth in the Spirit* (London: Burns and Oates, Ltd., 1966).

Section II

The Examen

A CHECK ON OUR AVAILABILITY
THE EXAMEN

A Positive Understanding of the Examen

The formal examen should be a time of prayer about
how much God has loved me in the very existential details
of my day, and how He could have loved me more in certain
situations if my inner spiritual decisiveness and external presence had been a bit different. This is not just a different articulation of the meaning of the Examen. Rather, it is a shift in
mindset that leads to an enormous difference attitudinally and
effectively. A healthy self-esteem has to be ultimately and irre-
vocable rooted in our Father's love, climaxed in His victory in
Jesus. This neither excessively highlights, nor denies, my daily
sinful weakness. Rather, it leads to a consoling humiliation,
found in a Father's forgiveness, that is constantly available
in Jesus as my personal savior. In this way, the daily effect
of my sinful condition is not to tear down self-worth but to
build up true apostolic humility, which itself is the source of
genuine self-esteem.

This positive understanding of the Examen helps avoid
another fallacy. Many times, the full, rich prayer of the consciousness examen shrinks into a quick, superficial reflection

over the day; and the five traditional elements of the examen, thus, collapse into the third element by itself—a general survey of the day's activities. The formal examen, however, was never intended to be just a quick thinking-over of the day. It is supposed to be prayer—within a fairly specific form, one related to the daily contemplation but not identical with it. And if the examen is to be chiefly about God's love for me, then gratitude should play a major affective role. Of course, it is the gratitude of a sinner who is at peace with the nothing he can do on his own because he is still wonderfully learning how the Father's love turns everything to good—even his own sinfulness.

The Examen as Essential to Availability

In the conclusion to his letter to the Society of Jesus on apostolic availability, Superior General Pedro Arrupe makes this statement:

> To become partly immobile through lack of availability on the part of individuals and the consequent fear of superiors to give them the missions called for by our apostolate today, [sic] would constitute a most serious threat to the very existence of our vocation . . . Ignatian availability is the guarantee and the *condition sine qua non* of our practice, which leads to salvation, and alone is of interest to the Society and the Church.[1]

A strong claim! My central point here is that the daily examen is the *primary* means to maintain this disposition of Ignatian, and indeed, of all apostolic availability. Even so, why should a brief period of prayer assume such great importance? This leads us to another insight often neglected in the past.

The *formal* examen-prayer, with its five elements, lasting (usually) about a quarter-hour, is always a means to the *informal* examen, which is a special faith-sensitivity that is with one all through the day. Often in our early years, we turn the formal examen-prayer into an end-in-itself, giving to it a rigid fidelity that corrupts its significance. Of course, it would be illusory to imagine that we can grow into living the informal examen-sensitivity without the early development of habitual practice of the formal examen and a continuing adaptation of our involvement with this type of daily prayer.

Through the informal examen, a person acquires a special ability for discerning (or examining) "presence" in everything. For Ignatius, this quality-presence was more important and extensive than the formal examen-prayer, inasmuch as this presence helps the person to recognize the grace of apostolic availability and flexibility that is being offered in every situation.

Apostolic availability is a profound faith experience that roots one's identity and security in God's love. When a person's security is too rooted in a job or a place, or even in a certain reputation, there results a stubborn rigidity that undermines his availability, just as availability can equally be undermined by a disordered need for change and variety—as when a person is so superficially committed that he really does not care whether he is changed or where he is assigned.

In that same letter, Father Arrupe points to some of the challenges for "apostolic availability" that are especially present in the new directions, institutional involvements, and types of service that are required in the modern world. What is fundamental, though, is that availability is primarily a readiness and sensitivity of heart, not simply a changing of job or place. In the heart of a person serving for many years in the same mission, there can be an availability that is very apostolic and invigorating—and often more difficult than the "availability" that leads to a new assignment. Apostolic availability and genuine perseverance in the same task or place are never opposed.

In the formal examen, we hold up our day to be seen against the light of God's love. Sometimes, this will be more instructive for us than was the experience itself. We may appreciate what we did not even see in the actual experience.

At other times, we can savor the depths implicit in our sensitivity to the actual experience of the day. The continuing informal examen makes us sensitive in every situation to a Father's love that is always available and makes us ready to respond in filial love to the Father's desire, as Jesus was— especially on Calvary.

At such a point of insight, we see how often our cowardice or disordered desires reveal us to be persons of the "Second Class,"[2] who seek to make *God* come to what *we* desire. This is precisely backwards: consolation and greater apostolic service are to be found in our coming to what God desires. The sensitivity of apostolic availability distinguishes the heart of a person of the "Third Class" from one of the "Second Class." The difference can become very subtle in one's interior affective life, but what is always at issue is nothing less than better service for the justice of God's kingdom.

Availability and Discernment

In our sinful human condition, apostolic availability does not at all come naturally to us, but often is born of our decision dealing with desolation in accordance with the principles of Ignatian discernment. The seven capital sins, as inner affective experiences (before we intentionally act on them), are each a type of desolate violence endemic to our sinful condition. They infringe on, and restrict the freedom of, our availability. In decisively going against this desolate violence,[3] we become interiorly available to God's loving and consoling attractiveness, which always frees us for whatever his Heart desires of us now.[4] In this way, Jesus' own decisive availability to His Father, in service to our world, is gradually born in our affectivity through our careful living, with all the subtlety of discernment, in the face of our inner, desolate violence. The daily examen is the most practical and regular means to practice this discernment for availability. Our *particular* examen could, then, focus on the flaw or weakness that now is most keeping us from this fuller apostolic availability.

What is that flaw or weakness? It is not so much something that we decide on, but rather what God will reveal to us in His loving concern that all of us should belong to Him ever more, totally. By responding to His call through the particular examen, and directing our attention and effort primarily against that flaw or weakness, we are allowing ourselves to be drawn more into the apostolic availability of Jesus where He and we best find the Father.

The Examen: An Action-Reflection Model

Apostolic renewal is not simply being able to get more done. Apostolic activity is not measured simply in quantity but must respond to the dictates of a wise sensitivity in the zealous lover of God. A certain degree of reflectivity is essential to the growth of this sensitivity. Although in the beginning, this reflectivity may seem labored and artificial, as one matures in the Spirit it becomes more integrated, less obvious, and part of the "presence" one has everywhere.

There is much talk about various action-reflection models to help renew our apostolic presence; and, indeed, some such model can be an essential instrument and method for apostolic religious formation from the novitiate outward. I suggest that the examen is precisely such an action-reflection instrument, one that is built right into our daily life, and capable of fostering apostolic availability as a whole way of life open to service to the needs of our world for God's greater glory.

In these models, we reflect on our experience, hoping that the reflection will lead us to better quality in our apostolic efforts. Hence, the reflection is never for itself, nor is it directed to a self-centered sanctification. Often in the past, the examen did not have an apostolic orientation, but practice of the examen, the separate steps of action-reflection-action integrate into a sensitivity of everything for the call of our Father's love, in whatever way He desires for His greater glory in our world.

Just as the routine and regularity of the daily order help to keep the contemplative monk attuned to God, so the examen can keep the apostolic religious, who is both active and contemplative, attuned to God's love, mortified by apostolic availability, to find in everything of this world a son's filial, loving service to His Father.

NOTES

1. Pedro Arrupe, S.J., *Apostolic Availability: A Letter of Father General Pedro Arrupe to the Whole Society, with a Covering Letter to All Major Superiors on Our Ministries* (Anand, India: Anand Press, 1971).

2. *The Spiritual Exercises of Saint Ignatius of Loyola*, 154.

3. Ibid., 319.

4. Ibid.

NOTES

Becoming God's Heart
for the World

To live contemplatively—indeed, to become whom we
contemplate—this is the invigorating experience, the hallmark
enterprise and adventure that human existence is all about,
that for which every human heart is longing. The magnetic
appeal of the wholly Beloved invites our hearts to a transformation that is never easy, but it is so intimately renewing as
to be almost irresistible. It is the very heart of love. Lovers in
their mutual contemplation are not always explicitly aware of
this process of self-transformation into which they are being
engulfed, but certain challenging moments can starkly reveal
the risky loss of self that is involved. And yet, the very attractiveness of the beloved provides conviction and motivation
to embrace this risk. In that magnetic moment, love seems
an opportunity not to be missed. But love's opportunity and
risk are also costly—and lovers finally know this. Indeed,
the cost involved in the contemplation of lovers strikes to
the profound level of self-identity. But cost what it may, the
beloved's attractiveness lures the lover on to surprisingly
new depths.

The beloved in our reflection here is Jesus Christ, our
God and Lord, our Brother and, finally, all our sisters and

brothers, especially those suffering across all time and space.[1] And contemplative transformation into this beloved is the fundamental process involved in, indeed it *is*, devotion to the Sacred Heart of Jesus Christ. It is also the process with which examination of conscience is concerned. And there, we have at once the premise and the product of this reflection. Both devotion to the Sacred Heart and examination of conscience have a long history in the Ignatian tradition; but they have rarely, if ever, been viewed in relationship to each other. Regular examination of conscience facilitates a transforming experience of one's own heart into the beloved of one's heart, the Sacred Heart of God in Jesus Christ.

In recent years, there have been attempts, both within the Jesuit heritage and within the whole Church, to renew the understanding and practice of examination of conscience and of devotion to the Sacred Heart. Examination of conscience is now more often called consciousness examen or awareness examen. In its renewed form, the examen continues to bless and sensitize the hearts of many busy believers to the loving presence of God in all daily life. And while much work has been done in developing a contemporary theological understanding of devotion to the Sacred Heart, perhaps the actual presence of the devotion is not so widespread as that of consciousness examen, or at least is not widespread among those who frequently make use of consciousness examen.

Renewing Understanding of Examen

In the renewed understanding of the examen, two insights are key. First, a much more positive perspective has corrected a past view that often deteriorated into an overly negative, moralistic understanding. Rather than highlighting the bad actions of a day, the examen gives a primary concern to what is primary: God's revelation, a steadfast love in Christ Jesus always inviting and invigorating our consciousness. Formal examen sensitizes our hearts to the presence of this love in the ordinary details of every day. Whenever this love is recognized and responded to, our hearts simply must come alive with joy and gratitude. So gratitude is the major element in the actual time of examen prayer, as it should also be in our daily lives of faith. And this gratefulness for the wonder of God's love stirs the heart to action. Gratitude becomes the chief motive from which all ministry pours.

As the examen begins to make our hearts more aware of God's perduring love, we also begin to recognize how often and how easily we can be oblivious to that love—or how subtly, yet quite stubbornly, we can refuse response to love. This realization, when faced honestly and not rationalized away, can, whether rudely or quietly, awaken our hearts with healthy guilt, with sorrow and repentance. This experience of guilt and sorrow is anything but pleasant. Yet, as an experience of God's love, it does purify us; it does transform us. And the effect of that experience can only be a bolder, freer, more wide-ranging apostolic service. Mature faith and discipleship cannot happen without this painful transformation in the humiliating experience of guilt and sorrow. As the repentant sinner encounters God's forgiveness in Jesus, sorrow is transformed into hopeful, vigorous gratitude—and a burning zeal to serve God's loving justice in our world. In this way, thanksgiving—the central driving force in the heart of any mature disciple of Jesus Christ—dominates the daily examen and fuels its impulse toward loving action.

A second insight that renews our understanding of the examen is the importance of the *informal* examen, as distinguished from, though obviously not unrelated to, the *formal* examen. The formal examen is a specific time and style of prayer. Never meant as an end in itself, this formal practice of examen should gradually spill over and infiltrate itself, as a special faith-sensitivity, into a person's daily life. And so, we come upon the informal examen: a way of living. The informal examen is a matter of who we are and who we are becoming, whereas the formal examen is a specific prayer we regularly practice. Thus, a regular practice of examen can lead to that self-transformation that makes possible a genuine faith-sensitivity of heart, a dynamic connaturality with the Beloved, which we are calling here "informal examen." This dynamic development of formal examen into informal, into a pervasive faith-sensitivity of heart, is crucial—crucial both to a proper understanding of examen itself and to its role in the human heart's deeply desired experience of love: our becoming whom we contemplate.

Daily Conversion in Faith

Jesus' ministry erupts publicly among the people in a great sense of urgency—a wholly new revelation of God's love and the need for reform of mind and heart, if one is to recognize and respond to that love. This theme is so clear at the beginning of Mark and in the synagogue scene of chapter four in Luke. This radical personal conversion of faith is often described in the Scriptures as a manner of repentance. As a conversion that will cost a whole lifetime, it continually involves the risking and sacrificing of a temptingly attractive but false, illusory self while radically true and radiantly new creation is born in a person's daily response to the quiet urgency of God's love. But no experience of merely passing excitement will suffice for this.

Nor can such repentance and radical change of outlook ever be reduced simply to our own planning and control. A strategy of clear-sighted tactics and of fierce determination will always prove futile all by itself. In fact, if not properly motivated and accompanied by grace, it can actually corrupt the very adventure of faith into something unwholesome and unholy. Without a genuine experience of the wonder of God's love, the Gospel call—the call by grace and favor to radical change—cannot be heard, and healthy repentance cannot happen. It is the attractive beauty and power of God's love that reveals the inadequacy and sinfulness of our condition and unleashes in our hearts a desire to be much more than what we now may be. It is in this way that the wonder of God's love reveals our sinfulness. And this profound truth, so capable of being misunderstood, is always the bedrock of mature spiritual life. God alone sees our sinfulness most clearly for what it truly is: a choice against love. And it is this God who calls us to intimacy in the beautiful revelation of Jesus come among us as forgiveness. Every detail of Jesus' life, most especially His dramatic experience on Calvary, stretches and stirs our hearts in hope for a new creation, a new life, a whole new self. But repentance, with its purifying pain and suffering, is the only way to this urgently longed-for newness.

An honest repentant acknowledgment of sinfulness in the face of such love is neither obvious nor easy because it cuts our consciousness in humiliation. The guilt, shame, and embarrassment that come in the wake of such an acknowledgment sting and singe our consciousness. In the presence of such love, they make our spirits blush. The pain and hurt will, most often and quite spontaneously, make us wary and seek to activate defense mechanisms such as the rationalizations of denial and the distractions, not of joy, but of pleasure. These are moments for careful discernment in the life of any believer. For the humiliating pain of acknowledged sin, as intended here, is not the result of some overly scrupulous conscience. Nor is it the unhealthy guilt of self-hatred. Rather, it is the purifying consolation—not desolation, but consolation, however scouring—the consoling experience of God calling us to greater love and life and faith. Despite the pain, therefore, this repentant blush of heart is a grace not to be rejected. It is essential to any mature faith, to any measured zeal for God's world, to any discipleship that hopes to brave the road's full distance.

The guilt that introduces our embarrassed, repentant response to God's great, tender love requires a brief description here. Much past experience of unhealthy guilt has understandably provoked the overreaction against, even a dangerous disregard of, all guilt as unhealthy. Though unhealthy guilt can surely plague and dishearten us, there is a guilt born of God. And it stings. But for the lover, it also signals the Beloved's presence, a very active presence, a redemptive consciousness, inviting greater intimacy in faith with God. Unhealthy guilt is always anxious, worried about self, excessively fearing punishment, preoccupied with failure, at times verging on despair in the face of some unrealistic perfectionism. But healthy, consoling guilt is always the result of an interpersonal love relationship. And it focuses the heart beyond the self, on the Beloved, in painful sorrow for the wound one's lack of love has caused. Healthy guilt does not despair, nor does it disrupt the deepest peace of the soul. Healthy guilt is always intimately and very positively related to encounter, a repentant sinner's encounter with God's forgiveness revealed and available now in a crucified Son's intransigent love.

In the Dying, a New Life

In the tense struggle of this inner guilt, shame, and sorrow, we usually become aware of the risk and high stakes involved. We must let go of a self, or some aspect of a self with which we have been enamored, perhaps for a long time. Something must die if the new is to be born. It is a mortifying experience, but as it is not a mortification simply of our own making, neither can the outcome of it be clearly grasped in advance. It is a moment of perceived high risk. And the helplessness of such a moment, when we are on the verge of letting go of what used to be and are not yet in possession of what will be, can profoundly daunt and agitate our spirit. Furthermore, it is in no way simply our own power and ingenuity that will create a different future. In the helpless and sorrowful awareness of our sinfulness, it is only an act of trusting abandonment of self, sometimes done in the dark aloneness of faith, that will allow the Beloved to gift us with God's holiness, our only true human future. A process of conversion that has begun in love leads now to even greater love as a beloved God, in that faithful promise which is the risen Jesus, defies all darkness and rejects absurdity and pain as the final word.

The heart of God revealed in Jesus excites our hearts with the invitation to a new and brighter future. But only a heart scoured clean in the humiliation of repentance can respond to that invitation. The issue is as profound as self-transformation and as hopeful as a wholly new creation. But without a mortified response to God's loving invitation and without a risky letting go of self, such a future remains simply tantalizing, cheap grace, illusion.

The forgiving love of God brings the process of repentance to a conclusion of lively gratitude, profound joy, and enthusiastic zeal for ministry. The sorrow of a forgiven sinner is not depressing, however painfully purifying. Neither is this sorrow obliterated by the joyous gratitude and zeal for service that realized forgiveness brings. Rather, the humility of a saved sinner, while not destructively focused on the past, never simply forgets the sorrowful memory of forgiven sin. One cannot help but wonder whether Peter, in the maturity of his joy, during his after-breakfast walk with the risen Jesus, did not once again find his eyes well up with tears as three awkward questions burned his soul with his own lonely truth, but burned it precisely for the sake of fidelity, the journey in companionship, and, yes, for the great holiness of Peter that lay ahead (Jn 21:15-19).

The new self, created in God's forgiveness, is always strongly characterized by a profound, joyful thanksgiving for a deed neither deserved nor gained through one's own accomplishment. This deed of forgiveness and the hope of a new and better future resonate strongly in the repentant sinner's heart, now riveted on the challenging beauty of God's forgiving love, found fleshed forever in Jesus on the Cross. And so, the whole dynamic of the First Week of the Spiritual Exercises propels a person to confrontation, to enlightenment and encouragement before this passionate experience of Jesus on Calvary. Having taken upon Himself the sins of all, this Son, anguished in an olive grove over the agonizing prospect of humiliating death, is able to renew that trusting abandonment of self that allows Him to find once again His dear Father. And His beloved Father blesses this anguished abandonment with a future of absolute fullness in Resurrection. In the face of such enlivening abandonment on Jesus' part, we can find the graceful encouragement needed for that surrender of self that repentance always demands.

It is at this moment that the graces of fidelity and perseverance take root in the forgiven sinner's experience. And so, Jesus' Death into the future of Resurrection stands faithfully, for all ages, as God's forgiveness. It gives graceful encouragement to all repentant sinners in this risky and humiliating process of self-transformation. The persevering faithfulness of this new creation, this new heart, will always depend on how profoundly, how pervasively transformed the repentant sinner is in the encounter with God's Word of forgiveness.

As we gaze on God's forgiveness in Jesus crucified, besides a lively gratitude and profound joy, our heart knows the expansiveness of a great desire for God in Jesus—an apostolic desire to give ourselves as Jesus did in ministry of God's forgiving justice. This desire at the end of the First Week continues to expand as the attractiveness of God's love in Jesus is revealed through the remaining weeks of the Exercises. God's Spirit and kingdom revealed so compellingly in Jesus become our whole-hearted desire. To live in daily imitation of Jesus, to serve as an apostle in whatever way God desires, becomes the very energy of our hearts. And yet, as the experience continues, this desire can stretch our hearts still further; we may be so transformed, we may, in such transformation, be so intimately identified with Jesus that we become and, in the thoroughly real way the mysticism of Baptism and Eucharist accomplish in us, we may *be* Jesus in and for our world. And so, the joyous thanksgiving of a forgiven sinner, so much more than a mere devotional satisfaction, sets our hearts afire with such desire for the new identity in Christ Jesus that we become mystical activists, heralds everywhere of the good news of God's transforming forgiveness.

Consciousness examen may play a role of special importance in facilitating such a process of radical conversion. The profundity and pervasiveness of the transformation depend in large measure on a regular practice of examen. And rather than putting a clear conclusion to the process of radical conversion, the Exercises provide enlightening direction for the further and continual deepening desire for this daily identification with Jesus. For this reason, as the formal Exercises conclude and move to become daily life, we are always left with an even greater need than before for regular examen, that we may continue the daily discernment of God's love converting us steadily into Christ Jesus our Lord.

Goal of Examen: Devotion to the Sacred Heart of God in Jesus

Long after the retreat experience of the Exercises is finished, regular examen keeps our heart sensitive and responsive to the attractiveness of the Sacred Heart of God in Jesus. As we have already seen, thanksgiving and sorrow are the two chief affections in faith of the examen—and the sorrow itself, as we have also seen, finds its fulfillment in thanksgiving. Thus, through its term of thanksgiving, regular examen mediates our conversion and growth into Christ Jesus.

Through the basic meaning of the examen, each believer becomes a concrete embodiment here and now of the Sacred Heart of God in Jesus. Consciousness examen, therefore, by facilitating the transformation whereby a serious believer and disciple becomes devoted to the Sacred Heart, is profoundly related to that same devotion. For in this sense of the word, *devotion* refers to the fundamental shape and orientation of a believing heart to the Heart of God in Christ Jesus. And this sense of devotion cuts far beneath—it does not necessarily deny but rather must root—any specific, traditional devotional details and practices.

The transformation of self whereby our hearts radically become devoted to the Sacred Heart accomplishes some perceptible results in our lives. Growing integrity of heart and Ignatian magnanimity gradually centers, unites, and identifies our whole person and presence in the world. An inner stillness, fanned to burning flame in God's own creative love, radiates an energy of recollection—a collectedness—that can meld our often fragmented faith into the strong, live organism of a life decisively for God.

Such wholeheartedness first gives enlightenment, then courage, toward a functional desire and choice in the direction of the "heavenly" things of consolation and away from the "earthly" things of desolation. These desolate "earthly" things live in our flesh as the seven capital, selfish impulses toward sin that the Christian tradition has known so well for centuries; whereas the "heavenly" things of God's consoling love are the opposite impulses that also live in our consciousness where the Spirit of Jesus invites and breathes their confirmation, their development in us, as virtues, as the very shape of our heart. In the interweaving complexity and tangle of our daily consciousness, we discover that the tempting experience of these capital impulses to sin is precisely the battlefield upon which the fidelity of our commitment and devotion to the virtuous heart of God in Christ is tested and strengthened. And so, it is usually by standing strong against the tempting intensity of lust that the virtue of chastity grows. It is by decisively acknowledging and carefully standing against the violence of desolate rage that the tensile strength of nonviolent gentleness is forged. The examen is daily involvement in the process of transforming the impulsive desolations of our consciousness into the deep, consoling devotion and virtue of God's Sacred Heart. Once again, we notice that it is precisely in the dying that the new is born. And what is newly born through these mortifying struggles on the inner battlefield of our heart—the heart of each of us and the communal, societal heart of each group, each social structure—always affects apostolic presence in the world, always decisively affects actions for or against God's justice as revealed in the loving Heart of Jesus.

Finally, this conversion into the Sacred Heart of God in Jesus does not displace our weakness with an arrogant sense of our own strength. No, just the opposite! Maturity in faith is always growth to grateful realization both of our weakness and of our dependence on God's love for everything. A steadfast belief in God's love does not replace human weakness. Rather, it helps us patiently to wait upon the Lord and to recognize and celebrate God's love bringing strength into our weakness. For God's power is at its best in our weakness.[2] It is a power that is needed, for becoming who we contemplate takes courage, even as it brings energy. It is high adventure, with a promised wage of persecution, to enter and be taken up into the affectivity of Jesus, God's countercultural heart for the world.

Consciousness examen, then, is not a way to greater, self-reliant strength. But its daily practice transforms us into the Sacred Heart. We may become whom we contemplate and, so, stand in this world as living witnesses, agents of love, inviting others into God's Heart in Christ Jesus:

> Come to me, all you who labor and are burdened, and I will give you rest. Take my yoke upon you and learn from me, for I am meek and humble of heart; and you will find rest for yourselves. For my yoke is easy, and my burden light. (Mt 11:28-30)

And one more time, we listen to the Beloved, becoming whom we contemplate: "Today this scripture passage is fulfilled in your hearing" (Lk 4:21).

> "The Spirit of the Lord is upon me, because he has anointed me to bring glad tidings to the poor. He has sent me to proclaim liberty to captives and recovery of sight to the blind, to let the oppressed go free, and to proclaim a year acceptable to the Lord." (Lk 4:18-19)

Through a companionship with Jesus made intimate and tender, strong and apostolically peremptory, through days and years of fidelity to the exam of consciousness, and through the dynamic energy continually released in the experience of forgiven sinfulness, we may come to the apostolic gift that the fidelity of the friends of God can know. In becoming whom we contemplate, we may devoutly, reverently, boldly, and with His thirst for justice become, each of us and together, in the Holy Spirit, God's own heart for the world.

NOTES

1. See Matthew 25:31-46.
2. See 2 Corinthians 12:7-10.

Consciousness Examen

Examen is a practice without much significance for many people in their spiritual lives. This is true for a variety of reasons, but all the reasons amount to the admission (rarely explicit) that it is not of immediate practical value in a busy day. All these reasons and their false conclusion spring from a basic misunderstanding of this spiritual practice. Examen must be seen in relationship to discernment of spirits. It is a daily intensive exercise of discernment in a person's life.

Examen of Consciousness

For many people today, life is spontaneity. If spontaneity is crushed or aborted, then life itself is stillborn. In this view, examen is living life backwards and once removed from the vibrant spontaneity and immediacy of the experience itself. These people today disagree with Socrates's claim that the unexamined life is not worth living. For these people, the Spirit is in the spontaneous, so anything that militates against spontaneity is not of the Spirit.

This view overlooks the fact that welling up in the consciousness and experience of each of us are two spontaneities, one good and for God, another evil and not for God. These two types of spontaneous urges and movements happen to all of us. So often, the quick-witted, loose-tongued person who can be so entertaining and the center of attention and who is always characterized as being so spontaneous is certainly not being moved by or giving expression to the good spontaneity. For people eager to love God with their whole being, the challenge is not simply to let the spontaneous happen but rather, to be able to sift through these various spontaneous urges and give full existential ratification to those spontaneous feelings that are from and for God. We do this by allowing the truly Spirited spontaneity to happen in our daily lives. But we must learn the feel of this true Spirited spontaneity. Examen has a central role in this learning.

When examen is related to discernment, it becomes examen of *consciousness* rather than of conscience. Examen of conscience has narrow moralistic overtones. Its prime concern is with the good or bad actions we have done each day. In discernment, the prime concern is with the way God is affecting and moving us (often quite spontaneously!) deep in our own affective consciousness. What is happening in our consciousness is prior to, and more important than, our actions, which can be delineated as juridically good or evil. How we are experiencing the "drawing" of God (Jn 6:44) in our own existential consciousness and how our sinful nature is quietly tempting us and luring us away from intimacy with God in the subtle dispositions of our consciousness—this is what the daily examen is concerned with prior to a concern for our response in our *actions*. Hence, it is examen of consciousness that we are concerned with here, so that we can cooperate with and let happen that beautiful spontaneity in our hearts that is the touch of God and the urging of the Spirit.

Examen and Spiritual Identity

The examen we are talking about here is not a Ben Franklin-like striving for self-perfection. We are talking about an experience in faith of growing sensitivity to the unique, intimately special ways that God's Spirit has of approaching and calling us. Obviously, it takes time for this growth. But in this sense, examen is a daily renewal of and growth in our spiritual identity as unique flesh-spirit persons loved and called by God in the inner intimacy of our affective world. It is not possible for us to make an examen without confronting our own unique identity in imitation of Christ before God.

And yet, so often, our daily examen becomes so general and vague that our unique spiritual identity does not seem to make any difference. Examen assumes real value when it becomes a daily experience of confrontation and renewal of our unique spiritual identity and an experience of how God is subtly inviting us to deepen and develop this identity. We should make our examen each time with as precise a grasp as we have now on our spiritual identity. We do not make it as just any Christian but as this specific Christian person with a unique vocation and grace in faith.

Examen and Prayer

The examen is a time of prayer. The dangers of an empty self-reflection or an unhealthy self-centered introspection are very real. On the other hand, a lack of effort at examen and the approach of living according to what comes naturally keep us quite superficial and insensitive to the subtle and profound ways of God deep in our hearts. The prayerful quality and effectiveness of the examen itself depend upon its relationship to our continuing contemplative prayer. Without this relationship, examen slips to the level of self-reflection for self-perfection, if it perdures at all.

In daily contemplative prayer, God carefully reveals to us the order of the mystery of all reality in Christ—as Paul says to the Colossians: "But now it has been manifested to his holy ones, to whom God chose to make known the riches of the glory of this mystery among the Gentiles" (Col 1:27). The contemplator experiences in many subtle, chiefly nonverbal ways this revelation of God in Christ. The presence of the Spirit of the risen Jesus in the heart of the believer makes it possible to sense and "hear" this challenge to order ourselves to this revelation. Contemplation is empty without this "ordering" response.

This kind of reverent, docile (the "obedience of faith" Paul speaks of in Romans 16:26), and nonmoralistic order-ing is the work of the daily examen—to sense and recognize those interior invitations of God that guide and deepen this ordering from day to day and not to cooperate with those subtle insinuations opposed to that ordering. Without that contemplative contact with God's revelation of reality in Christ, both in formal prayer and in informal prayerfulness, the daily practice of examen becomes empty; it shrivels up and dies. Without this "listening" to the revelation of God's ways, which are so different from our own,[1] examen again becomes that shaping up of ourselves that is human and natural self-perfection, or, even worse, it can corrupt into a selfish ordering of ourselves to our own ways.

Examen without regular contemplation is futile. A failure at regular contemplation emaciates the beautifully rich experi-ence of responsible ordering to which the contemplative is continually invited by God. It is true, on the other hand, that

contemplation without regular examen becomes compart-
mentalized, superficial, and stunted in our lives. The time of
formal prayer can become a very sacrosanct period in our
day but so isolated from the rest of our life that we are not
prayerful (finding God in all things) at that level where we
really live. The examen gives our daily contemplative experience of God real bite into all our daily living; it is an important means to finding God in everything and not just in the
time of formal prayer.

A Discerning Vision of Heart

When we first learn and practice the examen, it seems
stylized and artificial. This problem is not in the examen-
prayer but in ourselves; we are beginners and have not yet
worked out that integration in ourselves of a process of
personal discernment to be expressed in daily examens. This
should not put us off.

Examen will always be fundamentally misunderstood if
the goal of this exercise is not grasped. The specific exercise
of examen is ultimately aimed at developing a heart with a
discerning vision to be active, not only for one or two quarter-hour periods in a day, but continually. This is a gift from
God—a most important one, as Solomon realized.[2] So we
must constantly pray for this gift, but we must also be recep-
tive to its development within our hearts. A daily practice of
examen is essential to this development.

Hence, the five steps of this exercise of examen as presented in the *Spiritual Exercises* of St. Ignatius Loyola (#43)
are to be seen, and gradually experienced in faith, as dimensions of the Christian consciousness, formed by God's work
in the heart as it confronts and grows within this world and

all of reality. If we allow God gradually to transform our minds and hearts into that of Jesus, so that we become truly Christian through our living experience in this world, then the examen, with its separate elements now seen as integrated dimensions of our own consciousness looking out on the world, is much more organic to our outlook and will seem much less contrived. There is no ideal length of time arbitrarily set for each of the five elements of the examen when it is practiced. Rather, the examen is a daily organic expression of the spiritual mood of our hearts. At one time, we are drawn to one element longer than the others and at another time, to another element over the others.

The mature Ignatius, near the end of his life, was always examining every movement and inclination of his heart, which means he was *discerning* the congruence of everything with his true Christ-centered self. This was the overflow of those regular intensive prayer-exercises of examen every day. As beginners or "old-timers," we must understand both the point of the one or two quarter-hour exercises of examen each day—namely, a continually discerning heart—and the point of the necessary gradual adaptation of our practice of examen to our stage of development and to the situation in the world in which we now find ourselves. And yet, we are all aware of the subtle rationalization of giving up formal examen each day because we have "arrived at" that continually discerning heart. This kind of rationalization prevents further growth in faith sensitivity to the ways of the Holy Spirit in our daily lives.

Let us now take a look at the format of the examen as presented by St. Ignatius in the *Spiritual Exercises*, #43, but in light of these previous comments on examen as discerning consciousness within the world.

Prayer for Enlightenment

In the *Exercises*, Ignatius has an act of thanksgiving as the first part of the examen. The first two parts could be interchanged without too much difference. In fact, I would suggest the prayer for enlightenment as a fitting introduction to the examen.

The examen is not simply a matter of the natural power of our memory and analysis to go back over a part of the day. It is a matter of Spirit-guided insight into our lives and courageously responsive sensitivity to God's call in our hearts. What we are seeking here is that gradually growing appreciative insight into the mystery that "I am." Without God's revealing grace, this kind of insight is not possible. We must be careful not to get locked into the world of our own human natural powers. Our technological world poses a special danger in this regard. Founded on a deep appreciation of the interpersonal, the Christian in faith transcends the boundaries of the here-and-now with its limited natural causality and discovers a God who loves and who works in, through, and beyond all. For this reason, we begin the examen with an explicit petition for that enlightenment that will occur in and through our own powers but that our own natural powers could never accomplish all by themselves: that the Spirit may help us to see ourselves a bit more as Gods sees us!

Reflective Thanksgiving

Our stance as Christians in the world is that of poor persons possessing nothing, not even ourselves, and yet being gifted at every instant in and through everything. When we become too affluently involved with ourselves and deny our inherent poverty, then we lose the gifts and either begin to make demands for what we think we deserve (often leading to angry frustration) or blandly take for granted *all* that comes our way. Only the truly poor person can appreciate the slightest gift and feel genuine gratitude. The more deeply we live in faith, the more we become aware of how poor we are and how gifted; life itself becomes humble, joyful thanksgiving. This should gradually become an element of our abiding consciousness.

After the introductory prayer for enlightenment, our hearts should rest in genuine faith-filled gratitude to God for the personal gifts of this most recent part of our day. Perhaps in the spontaneity of the happening, we were not aware of the gift and now, in this exercise of reflective prayer, we see the events from a very different perspective. Our sudden gratitude—now the act of a humble, selfless pauper—helps make us ready to discover the gift more clearly in a future spontaneity. Our gratitude should center on the concrete, uniquely personal gifts that each of us is blessed with, whether large and obviously important or tiny and apparently insignificant. There is much in our lives that we take for granted; gradually, God will lead us to a deep realization that *all is gift*. It is only right to give praise and thanks!

Practical Survey of Actions

In this third element of the examen, ordinarily we rush to review, in some specific detail, our actions of that part of the day just finished so we can catalog them as good or bad. Just what we should not do! Our prime concern here in faith is

with what has been happening to and in us since the last examen. The operative questions are: What has been happening
in us? How has God been working in us? What is being asked
of us? Only secondarily are our own actions to be considered.
This part of the examen presumes that we have become
sensitive to our interior feelings, moods, and slightest urg-
ings and that we are not frightened by them but have learned
to take them very seriously. It is here in the depths of our
affectivity, at times so spontaneous and strong, and at other
times so shadowy, that God moves us and deals with us most
intimately. These interior moods, feelings, urges, and movements are the "spirits" that must be sifted through, discerned,
so we can recognize God's call to us at this intimate core of
our being. The examen is a chief means to this discerning of
our interior consciousness.

Discernment presumes a real faith approach to life—that
life is first listening, then acting in response. The fundamental
attitude of the believer is one who listens. It is to the Lord's
utterances that he gives ear. In as many different ways and
on as many varied levels as the listener can discern the word
and will of the Lord manifested to him, he must respond
with all the Pauline "obedience of faith." It is the attitude
of receptivity, passivity, and poverty of one who is always in
need, radically dependent, conscious of his creaturehood.[3]
Hence, there is a great need for interior quiet, peace, and passionate receptivity that attunes us to listening to God's word
at every instant and in every situation and *then* to responding
in our own activity. Again, in a world that is founded more
on activity (becoming activism), productivity, and efficiency
(whereas efficacy is a norm for the kingdom of God), this

faith view is implicitly, if not explicitly, challenged at every turn in the road.

Our first concern here is with these subtle, intimate, affective ways in which God has been dealing with us during these past few hours. Perhaps we did not recognize God's calling in that past moment, but now, our vision is clear and direct. Secondarily, our concern is with our actions insofar as they are *responses* to the calling of the Holy Spirit. So often our activity becomes primary to us, and all sense of response in our activity is lost. We become self-moved and self-motivated rather than moved and motivated by the Spirit.[4] This is a subtle lack of faith and a failure to live as a son or daughter of God. In the light of faith, it is the *quality* of responsiveness of the activity, more than the activity itself, that makes the difference for the Kingdom of God.

In this general review, there is no strain to reproduce every second since the last examen; rather, our concern is with specific details and incidents as they reveal patterns and bring some clarity and insight. This brings us to a consideration of what Ignatius calls the particular examen.

This element of the examen, perhaps more than any other, has been misunderstood. It has often become an effort to divide and conquer by moving down the list of vices or up the list of virtues in a mechanically planned approach to self-perfection. A certain amount of time is spent on one vice or virtue, and then we move on to the next one on the list. Rather than a practical, programmed approach to perfection, the particular examen is meant to be a reverently honest, personal meeting with the Holy Spirit of God in our own hearts.

When we become sensitive and serious enough about loving God, we begin to realize that some changes must be made. We are deficient in so many areas, and so many defects must be done away with. But God does not want all of them to be handled at once. Usually, there is one area of our hearts where God is especially calling for conversion, which is always the beginning of new life. God is interiorly nudging us in one area and reminding us that if we are really serious about life in the Spirit, this one aspect of ourselves must be changed. This is often precisely the one area we want to forget and (maybe) work on later. We do not want to let God's word condemn us in this one area, and so we try to forget it and distract ourselves by working on some other, safer area that *does* require conversion but not with the same urgent sting of consciousness that is true of the former area. It is in this first area of our hearts, if we are honest and open with God, that we very personally experience the fire of the Holy Spirit confronting us here and now. So often, we fail to recognize this guilt for what it really is, or we try to blunt it by working hard on something else that we may want to correct, whereas God wants something else here and now. It takes time for beginners to become interiorly sensitive to God before they gradually come to recognize the Spirit's call to conversion (maybe involving a very painful struggle) in some area of their lives. It is better for beginners to take this time to learn what God wants their particular examen now to be, rather than just to take some assigned imperfection and get started on it.

And so, the particular examen is very personal, honest, and—at times—a very subtle experience of the Spirit calling in our hearts for deeper conversion. The matter of the conversion may remain the same for a long period of time, but the important thing is our sense of this personal challenge to us. Often, this experience of God's calling for conversion in one small part of our hearts takes the expression of good, healthy guilt that should be carefully interpreted and responded to if there is to be progress in holiness. When the particular examen is seen as this personal experience of God's love for us, then we can understand why St. Ignatius suggests that we turn our whole consciousness to this experience of the Holy Spirit (whatever it may be in all practicality, for example, more subtle humility, or readiness to get involved with people on their terms, and so on) at those two very important moments in our day—when we begin our day and when we close it, besides the formal examen times.

In this third dimension of the formal examen, the growing faith sense of our sinfulness is central. This is more of a spiritual faith reality as revealed by God in our experience than a heavily moralistic and guilt-laden reality. A deep sense of sinfulness depends on our growth in faith and is a dynamic realization that always ends in thanksgiving—the song of a "saved sinner."

Contrition and Sorrow

The Christian heart is always a heart in song—a song of deep joy and gratitude. But the Alleluia can be quite superficial and without body and depth unless it is genuinely touched with sorrow. This is our song as sinners constantly aware of being prey to our sinful tendencies and yet, being converted into the newness that is guaranteed in the victory of Jesus Christ. Hence, we never grow out of a sense of wonderful sorrow in the presence of our Savior.

This basic dimension of our heart's vision, which God desires to deepen in us as we are converted from sin, is here applied to the specifics of our actions since the last examen, especially insofar as they were selfishly inadequate *responses* to God's work in our hearts. This sorrow especially springs from the lack of honesty and courage in responding to God's call in the particular examen. This contrition and sorrow is neither a shame nor a depression at our weakness but a faith experience as we grow in our realization of our dear God's awesome desire that we love with every ounce of our being.

After this description, the value of pausing each day in formal examen and giving concrete expression to this abiding sense of sorrow in our hearts should be quite obvious and should flow naturally from the third element of practical survey of our actions.

Hopeful Resolution for the Future

This final element of the formal daily examen grows naturally out of the previous elements. The organic development leads us to face the future, which is now rising to encounter us and become integrated into our lives. In the light of our present discernment of the immediate past, how do we look to the future? Are we discouraged or despondent or fearful about the future? If this is the atmosphere of our hearts now, we must wonder why and try to interpret this atmosphere; we must be honest in acknowledging our feelings for the future and not repress them by hoping they will go away.

The precise expression of this final element will be determined by the organic flow of this precise examen now. Accordingly, this element of resolution for the immediate future will never happen the same way each time. If it did happen in the same expression each time, it would be a sure sign that we were not really entering into the previous four elements of the examen.

At this point in the examen, there should be a great desire to face the future with renewed vision and sensitivity as we pray both to recognize even more the subtle ways in which God greets us and to recognize the Spirit calling us in the existential situation of the future—and then to respond to that call with more faith, humility, and courage. This should be especially true of that intimate, abiding experience of the particular examen. Great hope should be the atmosphere of our hearts at this point—hope not founded on our own deserts or our own powers for the future but rather, much more fully in our God, whose glorious victory in Jesus Christ we share through the life of the Spirit in our hearts. The more we trust and allow God to lead in our lives, the more we will experience true supernatural hope in God in and through, but quite beyond, our own weak powers—an experience at times frightening and emptying but ultimately joyfully exhilarating. St. Paul, in a whole passage from the letter to the Philippians (3:7-14), expresses well the spirit of this conclusion of the formal examen: "Brothers, I for my part do not consider myself to have taken possession. Just one thing: forgetting what lies behind but straining forward to what lies ahead" (3:13).

Examen and Discernment

When examen is practiced each day, it becomes an exercise that so focuses and renews our specific faith identity that we should be even more reluctant to omit our examen than our formal contemplative prayer each day. This seems to have been St. Ignatius's view of the practice of the examen. He never talks of omitting it, though he does talk of adapting and abbreviating the daily meditation for various reasons.

For him, it seems the examen was central and quite inviolate. This strikes us as strange until we revamp our understanding of the examen. Then, perhaps, we begin to see the examen as so intimately connected to our growing identity and so important to our finding God in all things at all times that it becomes our central daily experience of prayer.

For Ignatius, finding God in all things is what life is all about. Near the end of his life, he said that "whenever he wished, at whatever hour, he could find God."[5] This is the mature Ignatius, who had so fully allowed God to possess every ounce of his being through a clear, abandoning "Yes" that radiated from the very core of his being that he could be conscious at any moment he wanted of the deep peace, joy, and contentment (consolation) that was the experience of God at the center of his heart.[6] Ignatius's identity, at this point in his life, was quite fully and clearly "in Christ," as Paul says: "For his sake I have accepted the loss of all things and I consider them so much rubbish, that I may gain Christ and be found in him, not having any righteousness of my own based on the law but that which comes through faith in Christ." (Phil 3:8-9). Ignatius knew and was his true self in Christ.

Being able to find God whenever he wanted, Ignatius was now able to find that God of love in all things through a test for congruence of any interior impulse, mood, or feeling with his true self. Whenever he found interior consonance (which registers as peace, joy, contentment) from the immediate interior movement and felt himself being his true, congruent self, then he knew he had heard God's Word to him at that instant. And he responded with that fullness of humble courage so typical of Ignatius. If he discovered interior dissonance, agitation, and disturbance "at the bottom of the heart" (to be carefully distinguished from repugnance "at the top of the head"[7]) and could not find his true congruent self in Christ, then he recognized the interior impulse as an "evil spirit" and he experienced God by "going against" the desolate impulse.[8] In this way, he was able to find God in all things by carefully discerning all his interior experiences ("spirits"). Thus, discernment of spirits became a daily, very practical living of the art of loving God with his whole heart, whole body, and whole strength. Every moment of life was loving (finding) God in the existential situation in a deep, quiet peace and joy.

For Ignatius, this finding God in the present interior movement, feeling, or option was almost instantaneous in his mature years because the central "feel" or "bent" of his being had so been grasped by God. For the beginner, what was almost instantaneous for the mature Ignatius may require the effort of a prayerful process of a few hours or days, depending on the importance of the movement or impulse to be discerned. In some of his writing, Ignatius uses *examen* to refer to this almost instantaneous test for congruence with his true self—something he could do a number of times every hour of the day. But he also speaks of examen in the formal restricted sense of two quarter-hour exercises of prayer a day. The intimate and essential relationship between these two senses of examen has been the point of this whole essay.

NOTES

1. See Isaiah 55:8-9: "For my thoughts are not your thoughts, nor are your ways my ways—oracle of the LORD. For as the heavens are higher than the earth, so are my ways higher than your ways, my thoughts higher than your thoughts."
2. See 1 Kings 3:9-12.
3. David Asselin, S.J., "Christian Maturity and Spiritual Discernment," *Review for Religious* 27 (1968): 594.
4. See Romans 8:14: "For those who are led by the Spirit of God are children of God."
5. *A Hunger for God: Ten Approaches to Prayer*, eds. William A. Barry, S.J., and Kerry A. Maloney (New York: Sheed and Ward, 1991), 38.
6. *The Spiritual Exercises of Saint Ignatius of Loyola*, 316.
7. John Carroll Futrell, S.J., *Ignatian Discernment* (St. Louis: Institute of Jesuit Sources, 1970), 64.
8. See *Spiritual Exercises*, 319.

SECTION III

MINISTRY AND PRIESTHOOD

A HIDDEN SELF GROWN STRONG

"How great are your works, Lord! How profound your designs" (Ps 92:6). Believers down the centuries have nodded reverent assent to this great, beautiful, and awesome truth. Indeed, our sisters and brothers—the saints—bow to the very ground, in humility and praise. But for most of us, while our appreciation of the depths of God's love as the center of holy mystery is certainly real, it can so easily be taken for granted. Genuine experience of the mystery of God is never simply a matter of studied knowledge. It always involves the commitment that belongs to all holiness and the almost mystical fire of all deeply personal faith. So the profundity of the mystery of God's love mirrors a similar depth of the human heart; and, therefore, any superficial sense of God's presence must bespeak a superficiality in one's sense of self.

Even as God's love defies any full grasp of our mind, so the depth of the human heart stretches beyond all imagining. Rather, an appreciation of our mystery, made in the image of God's own, can stir an eager ministry of service rooted in a deep-hearted fidelity and stamped with a contemplative spirit of reverence and wonder.

Though this essay is concerned with the relationship between spirituality and ministry, its intent is more specific and precise. The analysis presented here is meant to describe a spirituality that must profoundly influence the presence and service of any minister. It is a hidden self grown strong[1] that can radiate inspiration, direction, and fidelity for ministry. So I want to look upon, in some small but hopefully useful way, the hidden depths of the human heart—not as a reality that stands forth on its own! Our deepest center is God's most precious gift to each of us; and so, there is no way it can exist on its own. Our deepest, truest center is relational: it is our identity in Christ, daily developing and urging us forth in a whole way of living and choosing for others.

Fidelity is always born in our deepest center, our identity in Christ. But getting some hold on this event and its conditions requires a distinguishing and then an inter-relating, of three different dimensions of human existence: external behavior, inner spontaneity, and what I call "the core of the soul." Describing the process of integrating these three dimensions of human existence highlights the need of a core sense of self if we are to deal with the serious contemporary issues of a minister's hidden self revealed and grown strong in God's precious gift of Jesus. Such faithfulness in ministry presumes the ability to withstand the interference of any embarrassed self-consciousness because of the development of a center of identity profound and incisive enough to pick and choose our way through the distracting complexity of our secular age.

Are You Simply What You Do?

Most people quickly, almost reflexively, would answer this question in the negative. But it bears some further investigation. The dimension of human life spotlighted here is behavioral and external. On this level, each day is filled with all sorts of activities. Some of these have been so well learned over time that they are habitual and involve very little, if any, explicit consciousness. From the deft maneuvering of knife and fork at a meal to driving a car to browsing a newspaper, the action is very real but not very reflective, nor costly, in terms of energy. But other activities require lots of reflective, concentrated attention: studying carefully, repairing the motor of a car, driving in very busy traffic. This behavioral slice of life is often more complicated and busy than most of us realize.

Because the activity of this level is external, it does not include some hidden interior reality. Rather, this behavioral dimension of life lies open for observation, at least for any who care to watch. Detectives attempting to piece together evidence for a compelling case against a reputed criminal know well this observable slice of human existence.

These actions—though very real, perceptible, and often consumptive of enormous energy—constitute nothing more than a superficial part of our being. In themselves, cut off from inner intentionality, these actions have very little meaning branded upon them. Once again, the detective example is instructive. Circumstantial evidence cannot, in itself, prove guilt and intention. Though behavior does not automatically carry its meaning within itself, we all know the tendency so quickly to base our judgments of others, and of ourselves too, on these superficial observable actions. "What you see is what you get" becomes a judgment that imprisons a person's identity in this behavioral realm and, thus, denies any deeper inner mystery. Is this not precisely the injustice of an easy judgmentalism: judging a person's whole identity beyond the limited evidence of external behavior? Though it does not make sense in a moment of careful reflection, how easy it is to subscribe to the belief that what you do *is* who you are.

Granting its superficiality, we cannot, however, overlook the important role of this behavioral aspect in Christian discipleship. The message of Jesus is clear and indubitable: a sincere loving of our brothers and sisters is precisely what reveals the genuineness of our faith. Both the letter of James and the first letter of John, together with some sayings of Jesus Himself, are frighteningly blunt about this point.

Are we simply what we do? Surely not. But a renewed awareness is needed if we are both to recognize the reality and importance of the behavioral dimension for what it is and not to squander the depths of human life by limiting its full significance to this superficial, obvious reality.

Too Deep for Words

Human living involves another dimension quite different from the behavioral one just described. This dimension may be called the core of the soul. It is the most profound interior part of every human person. As an aspect of identity potentially available to everyone, this core of soul does not automatically spring full-grown into existence. If we are to grow to maturity in our humanity and in our spirituality (two realities that can be distinguished but never totally separated), this interior center must develop into the most profound personal aspect of daily life. Developing this core of the soul requires careful cooperation, sometimes labored in painfully anguished struggle while, at other times, with an ease of consciousness so obvious as to be presumed.

This core of the soul plays a crucial role in the process of discovery of our true self in the beauty of Christ. The Holy Spirit of God leads us through the daily experience of life to an ever deeper sense of self, to an ever deeper revelation of Christ. A profoundly personal inner world is gradually revealed, acknowledged, and then laid claim to, though this whole process is much more one of receiving than of making. It is the receiving and welcoming of an enormously valuable gift. With unique beauty, this true self, like hidden precious treasure, awaits discovery and development. Deficient appreciation of this inner beauty and truth can mislead a person to ragged self-esteem, and even to a misshapen self-loathing. Something similar can also happen in our relationships with others. To perceive others in a similar prejudice against their inner beauty and truth can spark quick personal judgments that are uncharitably false and damagingly misleading. Without much development of the core of the soul, a person is superficial and quite unsure about self because he is unaware of the gift of inner richness given in Christ. This under-developed person often lives like a pauper, victimized by a dragging lack of confidence and unaware of riches begging to be discovered.

This inner core of a person has a profundity and a simplicity that is literally beyond words. The core of the soul is not a place upon which to take a stand; nor is it a thing to be grasped. To speak of the core of a person in such terms is very misleading. Our deepest center stretches far beyond what can be conceived in clear and distinct ideas and what can be fully expressed in words. As we grow in our appreciation of this personal center, its presence dawns, alluringly shrouded in mist and mystery. Such mysteriousness does not imply cloudy ambiguity. Rather, within the shifting mists of this inner mysterious realm, there can dawn a great quiet and clarity of vision. Allowing ourselves to be led further into this core of self facilitates a wonderful process of simplification. Life's complexities fuse into an undaunted simplicity. A noisy world hushes into a resounding quiet, and a polluted heart is stripped clear and clean. This core of the soul is marked by a simple calm and quiet beyond any cataclysmic storms and brutalizing temper tantrums. This deepest core of the soul speaks of the infinite simplicity of God and of love beyond words that is breathing life within us.

But such profound depth of personal center can also frighten people in a dizzying vertigo of two types. First, there is the fear of being trapped in a suffocating loneliness. Entering into their deepest center can easily confront people with the potential danger of a loneliness whose suffocating effect just does not seem worth the risk. For these people, discovering a greater sense of one's uniqueness seems inevitably to entail ever greater loneliness. Surely, loneliness is unavoidable and can, at times, swamp us in fearsome ways. But the same loneliness, when properly dealt with, can serve to teach the invaluable lessons of how precious our uniqueness is and, yet, how communitarian our personal identity is. In the core of the soul, no deadening loneliness sucks away the breath of life. Rather, in the core of our soul, God's creative love is breathing the gift of life into us moment by moment, now, and on into eternity. It is this same creative love, unique to each one of us, that breathes life into each and every person. And so, as we are led ever deeper into the core of our soul, our experience of God and of ourselves becomes ever more profound, personal, and unique. This God-centeredness is not meant to segregate each of us in a lonely solitariness, but rather to root and unite us in the community of the universal human family created in the image of God's Trinity. Finally, we are not, and never can be, alone.

A second fear can be even more frightening. After we know the potential for evil within ourselves, a question with ominous consequences can stare us to a standstill. What runs deeper within me: goodness or evil? It is easy to become so frightened by a potentially "evil" answer to my question that either I aggressively shun any deepening of self-discovery or I force and fabricate a "good" answer that is, finally, illusory and very unreal. Such a fear often plays itself out in a furious pace of busy distraction and empty activity. But such fear has often been addressed by God—and with a clarity unmistakable in the revelation of Christ. In the Catholic doctrine of creation and redemption, so often enunciated by the Church, God reveals that in every human person what runs deepest is the goodness of Divine love and forgiveness. There is in each of us a deep central point where evil cannot reach, and where only the beauty of God's creative love exists in all its uniqueness. Such continuing proclamation in the Church can quite fear and invite an evolving abandonment into our deepest truest self in the love of God that is Christ Jesus.

Are You Only What You Feel?

As with the similar question above about behavior, so this question would not win reflective assent on the part of most people. But this issue, too, bears some further investigation. The area of human experience delineated here I will name the "skin" of the soul. In obvious contrast to the core, the "skin" is not so profound and is, thus, more superficial. And yet, this skin-of-the-soul dimension is meant to name the very real area of spontaneity that registers in the human experience of all of us, either rationally of affectively. Though affectivity, sensuality, and other aspects of human spontaneity are rooted within the psyche, their result registers and is felt on the "skin." These spontaneities of thinking and feeling skitter their way across the skin of our souls, but never strike to the core. This level of human experience is distinct from the two previously described. Emotional, felt experience is not behavioral in itself, though it can be expressed in and motivate certain behaviors. The spontaneities of impulse, image, and mood can flail and rage across our minds and feelings with the intensity of an electrical storm. Such storms seem to come and go at times with a bedeviling arbitrariness that can frustrate and enrage us. But they do, finally, pass. These spontaneities, whether fiercely storming or quietly passing, are neither permanent nor profound. This level of spontaneous, unintended experience is characterized by unpredictable, shifting sands and is not capable of the rock-like dependability of the core of the soul.

Are we ever simply and wholly identified by what we spontaneously think or feel? The very profundity of human personhood answers this question in the negative. Spontaneities of thought and feeling are real and important phenomena of human experience. But the human person potentially runs deeper than any of these spontaneities. "What I feel" is never equal to "who I am." Because the core of the soul bespeaks a profundity not available to these spontaneities on the skin of the soul, we must, however, not assume that these spontaneities, both rational and affective, are any less real or any less important in the process of integration that is human and spiritual maturity. The point here is simple: these spontaneities happen on a different level of our person. As we shall see later, they find their direction only in relation to the soul's core.

Neither "what I feel" nor "what I think" ever fully equals "who I am." But confusion among these various statements about the self happens easily and is always dangerous. In reaction to a past spirituality that was too rationalistic, many of us are prejudiced to think that what we feel at any given moment is precisely and intensely who we are. This prejudice, whenever it tricks us, damages human and ministerial development because it short-circuits our relationship with God and it sideswipes the requisite responsibility and dependability for service.

Ministers, involved in so many different ways in the lives of other people, must come to a healthy human maturity and a reliable personal spirituality. All reliable ministerial spirituality for service involves a hidden self grown strong in the proper integration of the three dimensions of human experience here described.

Our Experience of God on These Three Levels

Some reflection on what the experience of God is like on these three levels can lay the groundwork for a description of the dynamics involved in their integration. Although we must be careful not to dissect human experience into a clarity that becomes unreal, it is helpful to notice that each of the three levels presented here correlates with a different type of experience of God. To confuse any of these levels and its correlative type of experience of God can produce serious misunderstandings—first, about our own relationship with God, but then also with implications for our ministerial service of others.

Our most profound and personal experience of God is in the core of our soul. The core's profundity is not given to intensely exhilarating experiences. Because the waters of our core identity run deep beyond words, God's love is not experienced there like the excitement of cresting and breaking waves of emotion. Rather, God's love resounds as a presence perduring and endearing. This profundity of God's perduring presence can produce an inner quiet—like the catching of one's breath—behind and beyond all exciting spontaneity and breathless activity.

At our deepest center, we are not actually *doing* or *feeling* anything. This is the point where we *are*—where we are in God, and are continually coming to be in the breath of God's loving spirit. This center of being, this presence, does not completely elude conscious grasp. Moments of prayerful reflection, sometimes carefully attuned to our breathing, can reveal a deep inner calm and quiet, which does not have a deadening effect but, rather, renews and enlivens. This is holy ground. In the holiness of this quiet sanctuary, with an attractiveness beyond imagining, God's love is grasping, laying claim to, and identifying each of us in Christ. It is the still point in the ever-turning world of our own person and of the whole cosmos. The gift of human freedom and personal responsibility is rooted in this profound point of our identity. Each of us has the capacity, at this profoundly personal level, to turn away from, to actually refuse cooperation with, such a foundational invitation of God's love. But it is we, not God, who can turn away, and with the resoluteness of life-or-death decisiveness. How astonishing, and yet how true, that we can so turn away! And yet, in such a central life-giving point of ourselves, God does not turn away. God cannot turn away, lest our very person be annihilated. Jesus Himself is God's promise of fidelity to our deepest truest person.

In contrast to the core experience that founds our very person, God's creative love touches us on the skin of the soul with a spontaneity and transitoriness that can be affective and rational. God's loving Spirit is felt—at times, with an emotional intensity and intimacy that moves us strongly and, yet, cannot perdure for long. Though it is an experience more transitory and superficial than that of the core of our soul, it is no less real, nor less precious as the gift of God. This spontaneous experience of God sometimes feels so different that it can easily distract us from that more profound and lasting experience.

The affective and rational fluctuation that occurs almost daily on this level of life includes a great variety of spontaneous experience. Special feasts and occasions can thrill us with the exciting intimacy of God's very personal love in us with the exciting intimacy of God's very personal love in Jesus. At other more ordinary times, a sudden touch of Divine love can surprise us in a moment of joyful ease and trust, thus transforming the humdrum into something momentarily special. But each of us also knows moments of felt absence when God feels distressingly distant. Finally, it is on the same dimension of ourselves where we experience impulsive feelings and thoughts that run directly contrary to union with God in service of others. The Christian tradition has studied and designated these experiences as the seven capital impulses to sin that stretch and strain, seduce and tantalize our consciousness into a selfishness that can feel sensuously delightful at times, but always dampens God's spirit of joy in our hearts.

This mixture of superficial spontaneity enfleshed in moods, impulses, images, and feelings must be carefully interpreted in faith because it importantly, if not always clearly, affects our experience of God. These experiences are unavoidable, and they are known quite differently than those of the core. As an unavoidable part of daily consciousness, these spontaneities must not lure us into unrealistic expectations. However, much as we may hope for such control, the choice simply to exterminate them is unreal. The real choice is whether we can recognize the attractive invitation of God's love in all this fluctuation—an invitation that stirs us in ways quite different from our core experience of God.

Finally, our experience of God also affects the behavioral level, in ways different from the previous two levels. Our daily activities can be part of, and deepen our relationship with, God; or they can interfere with, and even destroy, that relationship. The decisive issue is inner motivation. Behavior that is motivated by and actually expressive of our experience of God's love at the inner core or on the more superficial level of spontaneity becomes part of our personal love relationship with God. In this way, such behavior always unites people in Christ. On the other hand, external activity motivated by and expressive of impulses of selfishness somehow violates our relationship with God and effects, in some large or rather small way, a disruption and separation among people. The light of God's love, finally, always brings people together in unity, whereas the darkness of selfishness always splinters and divides.

Thus far, we have distinguished three dimensions of our human make-up, and we have briefly described the different types of experiences of God that happen on each of these dimensions. Already, the reader can see inter-relationships among our various experiences of God on these three levels. To identify ourselves with the experience of God on only one of the three levels is always a mistake. Such exaggeration impoverishes both our experience of God's love and our ministering of that love for others. And so, the most important challenge that God's attractive love invites any minister to is the integration of these dimensions into our whole and true self in Christ.

Dynamics of Integration

By describing some of the dynamics involved in integrating these three dimensions of ourselves, my desire is to present a realistic spirituality for busy ministers. My intention is not to present an analysis that may be clinically clear and exact but unrealistic, even unlivable, for busy servants of God's love. My concern all through this essay is with a spirituality that will hold up in the daily tensions of life and service, and will facilitate any ministering of God's endearing love in many other human hearts. It is a hidden self grown strong that anchors dependable ministry.

I will describe the dynamics of integration by presenting two basically different cases. In the first case, integrating the behavioral and the spontaneous with one's identity in the deep core of the soul is easy and almost effortless. We all have good days like this when life goes smoothly and being faithful to our truest self seems obvious and easy. If we analyze this experience of unreflective connaturality, we can appreciate just why it is so easy. In the first place, days of such easy integration presume a deep-down, reflective awareness, developed slowly and carefully over years, of the rightness of our core identity: as someone created in Christ and, thus, called to a particular state in life, whether it be marriage with this particular person, ministerial priest in the diocese, membership in a particular religious congregation or a specific dedicated, single lay life. This core identity, whatever its appropriate particularity, has developed gradually and come to be appreciated as a reality and consciousness involving more than the behavioral and superficially spontaneous levels. We know this identity touches something beyond what we are presently doing or feeling.

The reason that authentic living seems so easy on these days is that the spontaneous register of the skin of our soul is in obvious resonance with this developed core identity. Today, being who we truly are feels fine and seems easy. Therefore, the fleshing out of this core identity in daily actions of all sorts is also easy. The three levels of our person fall together in an integration focused by our unique core identity of Christ. To be and act in accord with being husband or wife in this marital relationship, today, has a smoothness and congruence to it that should not be distrusted. At such times, the spontaneities of mind and heart can be more readily trusted and followed because they are so obviously in line with our deepest identity. The faith interpretation of the rightness of such congruence is too obvious to be doubted.

But there is another case in which the process of integration is quite different. It is anything but smooth and easy. On these days, being true to our God-given identity in Christ is fraught with confusion, temptation, and excruciating challenge. Something has mightily shifted from the previous connatural experience of integration. More than just a different day, this situation seems like a whole new world. And we feel like a completely different person. The previous clear identity has now been shaken way out of focus. What could possibly explain such a difference? It is precisely at this point where serious, careful interpretation in faith is required. And any misunderstanding here would have serious implications, not only for our own personal relationship with God in Jesus, but also for our ministerial presence to others.

What has changed here is not my deep core identity, but the spontaneous fluctuation on the skin of my soul. Though my whole person may feel different, the core identity revealed and developed over time, and previously so clear, holds true—however much it may see out of focus now. The confusion and ambiguity of such a time is provoked by a change in the spontaneity of how I am thinking and feeling about who I am. Something I have done may have caused this shift or it may simply be due to the unavoidable fluctuation built into our human condition on this level. Regardless, how to act and to be my truest self in Christ now is not obvious. Careful reflection and decisive dynamics become crucial at this point.

In such a situation, I do not feel an attraction for my deepest identity. In fact, there may be a positive distaste for what had previously been so attractive. For example, the special intimacy in faith of God's love in Jesus and the energetic desire to live and share that love that had characterized a celibate commitment may now be suffocated in a dissecting loneliness. As mentioned above, such a shift could be caused by irresponsible activity on my own part. But it can also simply be part of passionate human living with its vagaries and fluctuations that challenge and invite deeper and more personal commitment to my core identity. Rather than the easy integration previously described, the three levels of my person now feel as though they are in direct collision with one another. The stress and strain of this collision tempts my vocational commitment and invites a more personal and profound profession of my core identity in Christ.

In such a vocationally challenging time, my core identity remains deep and true. But such truth is camouflaged in the confusing shift of spontaneity on the skin of the soul. And so, it becomes a matter of great importance to ferret out this identity in Christ and to live and act in clear decisive presumption of this precious, though now hidden, gift. This presumption of previous identity is not vague and elusive, like clutching at fog. Rather, it is a terribly important, personal act of belief in a gifted identity that has been previously revealed and developed over the years, however confused and hidden it may now seem. And such a personal act of faith must then be enfleshed in an appropriately courageous gesture.

At such a time of vocational testing, I cannot simply trust and follow the spontaneous flow of my feelings and thoughts because now they are in opposition to my deepest, truest identity, as revealed and professed in Christ. This does not mean that I can simply disregard such spontaneity in an unhealthily repressive way. What is needed is precisely an honest facing and interpretation of these experiences. Because such thoughts and feeling in their spontaneity cannot validate themselves, they will need to be tested and interpreted against my core identity.

While the soul's attention is seductively engaged with distracting images and enticing moods prancing across the stage of my consciousness, a sense of core identity is no longer center stage and can seem quite removed, if not unreal. So, first and foremost, I must exercise some courageous detachment from these superficial, yet intensely absorbing, experiences. This detachment is motivated by a faithful presumption in favor of my previously professed identity. Such detachment is not an outright denial of reality nor a repressive withdrawal from the importance of these contrary spontaneities. It simply provides some space and time for restoring perspective. But it often requires quite a strength of practical conviction to move against this veritable tidal wave of contrary emotion and, thus, prevent its suddenly flooding out the bastion of my previous identity so as to assume, on its own, the importance of a whole new identity. Yet contrary feelings and thoughts are disguised in precisely that fashion.

But identity must always be something more profound and continuous than images periodically flashed on the soul's screen. This courageous stepping back from the intensity of the present spontaneity makes possible renewed acknowledgement of my core identity. This renewal is not some slight fleeting nod but should be as full-hearted a remembering as possible. Contemplating some past wedding pictures, studying a few pages of personal journal description, or listening to the tape of one's final religious profession ceremony can begin to renew and personally enliven memory, calling to mind a core identity previously revealed and professed in Christ. This renewal of identity is of paramount importance because it serves as a steady compass to find direction in the present gusts of contrary winds. To have allowed one's previous identity to run cold, and even to die, is to find oneself painfully marooned and battered in the gusty experience we are here describing. Sometimes this process of concrete renewal of identity rather quickly changes the weather of the soul, cuts the wind out of the sails of the present emotion, and, thus, brings a settled calm and stability. But even if the change is not so sudden—and usually it is not—nonetheless, such renewed awareness of core identity now allows me to interpret the present state of affairs from the midst of a renewed identity in Christ rather than from the position of being swamped and up-ended in the present wave of emotion and thought.

Interpretation from this renewed core of soul facilitates deciding and living from this deepest center. Believing in a hidden self brings strength and provides direction. Just as, in the first case considered, the consonance of spontaneity on the skin of the soul with my identity in the core reveals the grace and love of God in the spontaneous experience of that moment, so in this present case, the dissonance and opposition, when honestly faced, crystallize a different interpretation. This lack of consonance between the present spontaneity and my core identity reveals the misguided, tempting nature of the present thought or feeling. The invitation is loud and clear for those who want to hear: to stand strongly against this gusty onslaught and act and live out of my deepest center. Only in this way and with the presence of these dynamics will I achieve an integration of the three dimensions of my person. On days such as these, the integration struggled for prevents the collision of these dimensions from shaking loose my personal identity from the moorings of my deepest center. A hidden self has grown even stronger.

Much of our life is spent enjoying the consonance of present spontaneity with core identity. And these many times of more obvious correlation instruct us in valuable ways about God's faithful love inviting our own faithful loving response, as much as do those times of agonizing vocational testing. But the latter can have an intensity and challenge that enshrines them with special value along our life's journey into deeper transformation in Christ. However painful and excruciating the onslaught of stormy weather may be on the skin of the soul, to have stood firm and true to my deepest self in Christ rewards me with increased confidence and self-knowledge. But it brings an even more precious result: a more trustworthy and personal conviction about God's faithful promise to stand firm to the gift of my identity. Jesus as risen Lord is that promise. And so, both the ecstasy and the agony of living God's deepest truth teach and encourage us.

Contemporary Critical Importance of Mature Core Identity

The central thrust of this whole essay highlights the tremendous importance of the core of the soul for all mature human living. The validity and effectiveness—indeed the very possibility—of the two cases previously described with their correlative dynamics for integrating the three levels of ourselves depend upon a developed core of soul. Our very identity, and its continuing development, must be founded in a dimension of ourselves that runs deeper than the superficial levels of spontaneity and activity. Our identity cannot be something chameleon-like with a fresh new face for each day of the week. In fact, it is precisely a profoundly settled identity that makes possible the personal flexibility and adaptability required for the challenges of much contemporary ministry.

Such a developed core identity in the minister is always necessary for spiritual identity and dependable ministry. But, for three reasons, this core identity assumes critical contemporary importance. In the first place, it is precisely this inner core, this hidden self grown strong, that provides any assurance of fidelity to promises and commitments, great and small. This reminder becomes especially important in an age like our own, when fidelity is so rarely spoken of and, according to some observers, has such a poor track record among us to be calling us, perhaps, to a whole new discovery and understanding of faithfulness. Without a developed sense of identity in our core, promises and commitments are rootless and too easily disposable. The unpredictable fluctuation of spontaneity in our hearts can not only bewilder us but can also frustrate us in a confusion that undercuts the inspired courage needed if we are to be people ministering in fidelity to the promise of our word. The excitement and competition of our fast-moving, busy lives will not only wear us down in fatigue but easily lure us away from the prayerful reflection needed to discern and preserve the basic continuity involved if we are to be faithful to our God-given identity in Christ. For anyone whose person is played out simply on the levels of behavior and spontaneity, the continuity and tenaciousness of faithful identity become impossible.

This issue of faithfulness to promises and commitments, especially to a commitment of identity—profoundly personal beyond any work, career, or individual project—remains a serious concern of our times. This issue of fidelity to promises and commitments raises questions about how we profess in public our deepest personal identity in Christ. This essay is not the place to answer these questions. But just to articulate some of the questions here can, perhaps, invite the conversation about them needed among us for more insight and clarity regarding them. As we mature in life and faith, how do we recognize and then publicly profess before God, in the Church and contemporary society, the permanent identity revealed in our deepest center? What is the rationale that helps the one professing, the Church, and contemporary society to understand this process of profession in a sufficiently similar sense for it to have real meaning and to become the critically needed foundation for all faithful love and relationship in our world? How can this process of profession and its rationale of understanding create similar expectations of faithfulness on the part of all the parties involved? How do these similar expectations of fidelity encourage an ongoing development of identity for us all? How does this publicly professed inner identity, and our similar expectations of it, become a profound resource to fall back on, providing guidance and direction, especially in times of crisis, but also over the long haul of our lives?

These questions about public profession of and fidelity to our identity bring us smack up against many secular forces in western society that strongly militate against such professed fidelity. And the increased intensity today of such secular forces, whether overtly militant or more subversively present, is the second reason why the core of the soul assumes such critical importance at this time. In a Styrofoam world, practically everything becomes disposable. In a world of universal advertising, carefully crafted and overly idealized models send us in mad pursuit of personal ideals that are utterly unrealistic. In a highly technologized world, computerized programming can lure us into the myth of immediate fulfillment and accomplishment. In a highly mobile society so often characterized by the transient, the developmental, and the temporary, where can we find encouragement and help for the patient perseverance always needed for faithfulness? In a highly competitive world, enormous effort to prove the self creates a breathless tension that finally deflates any value and belief in self. In a world that respects only what it can measure and get its hands on, the core of the soul seems elusively unreal—some figment of the imagination.

These aspects of our age defy the belief, the hope, and the patience needed to recognize and live faithfully in accord with God's loving revelation of the precious gift of our truest self in the core of our soul. As people chosen, identified, and specially blessed in the saving blood of Jesus, our only way of avoiding enslavement to this pernicious secular spirit of the world is to develop a profound durability of self—a durability and depth at our core that is at once rooted against the onslaught of secularism and, even more importantly, sensitized for recognizing God's Holy Spirit of creative love at work in this same world.

A third reason for the contemporary importance of core of the soul is the special need that western society has now for a profound self-consciousness. Though this overlaps a bit with the first reason above, it warrants, in my opinion, separate development here because of its implications for ministerial spirituality. A growing number of commentators on our western culture are concerned about the loss of a profound sense of self. In the enormous cultural shifts of the past fifty years or more, while life was changing remarkably for everybody, this deep, central sense of self, often serving like a rock-fast lighthouse on a stormy night, has been darkened.

No one explicitly planned it this way. Rather, something happened almost without our noticing. The light is out. A compass has been lost. A rocky foundation has washed away. Whatever image is used, the reality is the same.

Walker Percy, the American southern essayist and novelist who died in 1990, in many of his works pointed in different ways to this critical loss of self-consciousness.[2] The self-consciousness, whose loss in western culture Percy bemoans, is a reality of the core of the soul.

Clearly, the meaning of self and of self-consciousness used in this essay is something very different, indeed, from the term, "self-conscious," as used in contemporary American parlance. We speak of feeling "self-conscious." This self-consciousness is a superficial experience felt on the skin of the soul. Its spontaneity rattles us with an awkwardness that throws us off our pace and disturbs our natural response. This feeling of self-consciousness, though it often sets off an alarm of inner awkwardness, is usually provoked by an unfriendly reaction imagined on the part of other people, whether present or not. Because of how we think others do or would react to us in a certain situation, we feel self-conscious. The self-consciousness briefly sketched here is superficial, not a matter of the core, and yet can seriously disturb our equilibrium and corrode our presence to others. In this way, it can spontaneously and strongly interfere with, and actually prevent, our ministry of service to others.

Only a profound consciousness of self developed deep in our core can prevent this superficial self-consciousness from rattling our presence in a way disturbing to our ministry to others. In this brief treatment, two quick points are needed to avoid misunderstanding. This awkward self-consciousness is an inescapable part of our human condition and, so, is not meant to be completely avoided. And it is not always something bad and interfering; it can, at times, have a beauty to it and be a graced stirring of our spontaneity. But it is only a core sense of self that can interpret these various experiences of self-consciousness and prevent them from being too determinative of our person and our ministry. Without such deep-centered self-consciousness, we can become a reed, not only blowing in the wind, but rootless and easily broken off—and finally, without much dependability for ministry.

How do we in the West regain the profound sense of self that must underlie and that can withstand the harmful influence of a socially induced self-consciousness? Obviously, no simple, quick answer awaits that question. It will require lots of study, reflection, and discussion among us all. It is clear to me, however, that what I am here calling the core of the soul will play a critical role in any adequate answer and that this core must root any ministry of daily living and serving in a deep-hearted identity and intimacy in faith—an intimacy resonant with Jesus' own faithful intimacy with His dear Father.

Means That Help Develop the Core of the Soul

Granting the special contemporary importance of mature core identity, we will conclude by reflecting briefly on some means that can foster the development of our person over time beyond the behavioral and skin-of-the-soul levels. In the face of our age's excessive stress on spontaneity and activity, how does a person make the breakthrough needed to push beyond more superficial dimensions and develop a sense of self rooted in the core? I will mention three helpful means:

regular solitude, prayerful reflection, and an affective darkness in ministry that invites deeper faith.

Solitude as time spent alone with God and with oneself will always, sooner or later, test our sense of self and experiment with the central depth of our person. Solitude plays an essential role in moving beyond the levels of busy activity and superficial spontaneity. In these quiet times alone, if regularly planned and not just fitted to our moods and feelings, we can break through to a new level of experience and relationship—a whole new depth of peace—with ourselves and with God. Though we may squirm and doodle, dawdle, even seem to fritter time and ourselves away in the empty quiet, and often come upon feelings strange enough to occasion misgivings about ourselves and about God, nonetheless, solitude can bring us to a whole new kind and quality of presence in faith. It is a being with and in God, so simple as to be symbolized in the rhythmic breathing of God's life and love within us.

Various methods of self-reflection can also assist this movement to the center. Consciousness Examen, journal writing, and spiritual direction are just some examples of interiority, of a regular reflection that helps us to search for—and to receive—something underneath the busy flow of activity and superficial spontaneous fluctuations in our consciousness. Specific life experiences often invite that second look of reflection and, thus, have the potential for calling us deeper into ourselves. Dissatisfaction, frustration, and boredom with a life that is superficially being played out only on the levels of activity and spontaneity can invite many people either to the escape of a flurry of distraction or to something quite different: a moment and eventually, a life of deeper—even

Marian—pondering. Sometimes, responsibility calls us to a fidelity of action or presence that is, in the moment, directly opposed to what we are feeling. Such moments often face us with a more fundamental choice than we realize. While we can either outright shirk our responsibility or feel trapped in a stoical fatalism, we are also always capable of something else more bright and shining than all the previous: the joy of a deeper, more personally chosen freedom in our responsibility. These and many other experiences in our lives invite a deeper, more personal, entry into the mystery of ourselves. For example, surely friendship, being the cooperative venture that it is, has its own special ways of inviting lover and beloved into the precious discovery of new life and ever more beautiful identity in one another, and in Christ.

Solitude and prayerful reflection can especially help us to recognize in a peculiar darkness and affective dryness invitations to root our ministry deeper in the core of ourselves. We all know experiences in faith when we spontaneously feel what we believe. The skin of our soul is excited by God's love with a tangibility that is hard to deny. But we also know those other experiences when our belief about God's personal love leaves us unmoved, without any felt excitement, at times without any feeling at all. These moments, however unavoidable they may be in our maturing in faith, can easily be misunderstood. It is easy to lose belief in God's love simply because, "I don't feel it anymore." For one living on the skin of the soul, the felt experience in itself, unreflectively, becomes ultimate legitimation of the presence or absence of one's faith. But the reality is otherwise: we must learn to recognize the loving hand of God, at times dulling our sensuous, felt experience of love, precisely as an invitation to believe in a love far beyond what we feel. This becomes an essential element, however anguished and barren it may seem, of our growing up in faith. Unless this lesson is learned, our faith cannot be maturely founded in the core but will unpredictably wax and wane with the shifting tides.

This experience of affective dryness as invitation to deeper faith has its counterpart in a darkness of felt uselessness and failure in our ministry. These moments contrast sharply with the times of great satisfaction in the awareness of all that we are able to accomplish as instruments of God's transforming spirit. In these latter moments, God's love feels close, inspiring just the right words and actions. And we relish being able to see and feel such graced results. But ministry is not always so naturally enjoyable. Whether occasioned by a change of ministry or just perduring a long time in the same ministry, now we do not feel very inspired. And we do not seem to be appreciated much by those whom we are serving. Our ministry in the marketplace has darkened; and on the skin of our soul, we feel failure, monotony, and darkness.[3]

This darkness in ministry is an important moment for careful interpretation. If we do not too quickly opt out of the situation, it can root our understanding and practice of ministry more deeply in faith in the core of our soul beyond naturally satisfying feelings. After we have investigated as realistically as we can whether we are responsible for the sense of failure and uselessness, we must be careful not to presume that the reality in faith of our ministry is as it seems and feels. Mature ministry always believes in human cooperation. But mature ministry is also always learning to rely ever more fully on God's powerful love in Christ as finally much more transforming of our world than is our own activity.

This ministerial darkness can purify us as instruments for God's ministry of accomplishment far beyond what we can see and feel. But this time of anguished darkness in ministry, when misinterpreted, or simply avoided, keeps us immature as cooperators with God's dear love ministering in our world. Without the lesson this ministerial darkness can teach us, our ministry will not be dependable enough because it is not maturely enough founded in a hidden self grown strong in our soul's core. And failing this ministry, the quality of our presence in ministry will fluctuate unpredictably in accord with our feelings of satisfaction and fulfillment—and their contraries.

This process of personal development and ministerial maturing into the core of ourselves obviously happens over years. And we need help with such formation of self, today especially, because of some of the secular forces of our world mentioned earlier. The importance and difficulty of this kind of mature faith development poses some serious questions for programs of religious formation that prepare for permanent vocational choice and ministry. Whether we are speaking of preparation for marriage, for priestly ordination, or profession in religious life or for some other form of dedicated single lay life, the questions are the same and the issue is precisely a religious formation. How does the candidate for such vocational profession know that the call and response are being experienced in the core and not just in the present feelings in the skin of the soul? Where can he or she turn for help in this important process of self-reflection and understanding? What should candidates be experiencing in the core, as well as knowing that it is an experience in the core and not some more superficial part of the self, before the Church ratifies their vocation and commitment? Pre-Cana, seminary, novitiate, and other diocesan training-program personnel must continue to articulate answers to these questions in their programs and then facilitate such development with the candidates themselves.

The relationship of spirituality and psychology is a very current and thorny issue in our times. Without having made overt reference up to this point, I am aware that this essay's subject matter intertwines itself very much with this important contemporary relationship. The importance and subtlety of this relationship is heightened in an age such as ours in which our attention is so focused on the therapeutic and the individualized dimensions of human living. The conclusion of this essay is not the place to introduce and to treat this topic. But it does seem honest and appropriate to conclude with a few questions that can help us all rethink the various points of this essay and, perhaps, get some further insight into the important distinction between and integration of spirituality and psychology. One of the dangers in a time so colored by therapeutic language is that of a subtle, unintended selfishness. Concerns about "taking care of myself," "being good to myself," and "being faithful to myself" can narrow the gaze of our hearts in a selfishness too inwardly turned. This excessive self-centeredness becomes unhealthy and stymies a generosity naturally geared to the self-oblative dimension of Christian love and service.

What signs distinguish a so-called faithfulness to self that is really unhealthily selfish? And what signs characterize a faithfulness that can let God's love energize and stretch our generosity in ways that do not always feel good or immediately seem to be a clear development of our own individual self? These questions have no easy resolution and require honest, careful discussion. But there should be no doubt about the importance of such questions in relation to the strengthening of our hidden selves in Christ and the increased faithful service in the Church of maturely insightful, generous ministers.

Though I have stressed in these final sections the importance of a developed core of the soul for any busy minister, the central point of this whole essay should not be overlooked. Living and choosing from our deepest center is always a matter of integrating in faith the three dimensions of our person. This integration, when easy and when difficult, results in effective ministry to others. This integrated involvement of our whole person is never simply a matter of trained expertise in self-help personalism nor a process of determined application of practical techniques and strategies in various situations. We are really speaking of that interpersonal love affair with God in Jesus that gradually reveals the beauty of a whole new self, a hidden self grown strong. This constantly creative love strikes deep to our core, stirs a magnetism of spontaneous desire in each of us, and is finally *done* in courageous dependable ministry that continues the renewal of our world in the beauty of God's dream: Jesus.

NOTES

1. The phrase is Pauline. See Ephesians 3:16.

2. A recent biographer powerfully centers on Walker Percy's problem and achievement: "Percy's real work in fiction began when he gave free rein to those demonic voices raging within him, where he allowed his lack of a central or integrated self to become his real subject . . . Percy's imagination is most impressive in its power to show how we are quite literally constructed by our social and cultural ideolects. The awareness can lead to a psychological version of nihilism, a frightening conviction that we are nothing more than the sum of those discourses that constitute our consciousness. Percy himself had long been plagued by such nihilism, and even with the assurance of his faith he could never completely overcome it. The crucial thing about Percy's faith, though, was that it gave him hope that among the medley of discourses there was one that carried truth and authority . . . Discerning this language, finding and heeding this 'news' . . . was the one thing that could rescue the individual from the internal Babel . . . " See Jay Tolson, drawing in work of Michael Kobre, in Tolson's *Pilgrim in the Ruins. A Life of Walker Percy* (New York: Simon and Schuster, 1992), 279-80. Percy himself states the issue well in "The State of the Novel: Dying Art or New Science?" in Walker Percy, *Signposts in a Strange Land*, Patrick Samway, ed. (New York: 1991), 181 and throughout. For anyone wishing to pursue in depth this contemporary theme of self-consciousness, Charles Taylor offers massive, challenging guidance in *Sources of the Self: The Making of the Modern Identity* (Cambridge, 1989).

3. See Thomas H. Green, S.J., *Darkness in the Marketplace* (Notre Dame: Ave Maria, 1981).

A DIOCESAN PRIEST'S OBEDIENCE

Obedience and authority, especially today, are frequently found to be a partnership in faith that is strained—even nervously distrustful. In such an uneasy alliance, either partner can be a threat to the other in a way that disrupts unity and enervates zeal for service. An authoritarian command to "be quiet and do what you are told" hardly invites mature response and partnership. Nor does the arrogant charge that "nobody is going to tell me what to do" invite responsible dialogue and interaction with religious authority. In recent years, the interpretation and practice of obedience and authority have vacillated easily—sometimes abruptly— between these extremes. The reasons for such a tense, vacillating relationship are often obvious. Nonetheless, to capitulate to such a tension or simply to give up the struggle for any balance in this partnership in faith has serious effects on the corporate identity and mission of active apostles in the Church, priests.

Diocesan priestly obedience should always be oriented to corporate unity and corporate service within a presbyterate. Undoubtedly, what is here described is already being practiced in some dioceses to a greater or lesser degree; but beyond certain practices in different dioceses, what is needed is an explicitly recognized, consciously articulated, and, therefore, (at least in most cases) new conceptualization of diocesan priestly obedience.

Obedience and Today's Culture

In the book *Megatrends*, in which he describes ten new directions that are transforming our lives, John Naisbitt delineates a persistent development toward decentralization over centralization, toward participative over representative democracy, and toward horizontal networking over vertical hierarchy. In the Catholic Church as a whole, and in most dioceses, the effects these megatrends have had since Vatican II are clear for all to see. And although these more participative, decentralizing developments at first brought confusion and consternation, it is now clear that in many ways, they have enriched and renewed our faith as a Church, as well as our compassionately decisive involvement in the modern world.

But these secular trends and developments, as they continue to influence us as believers, also raise some serious questions of identity: What does it mean to be a Church? What does it mean to be a diocese? Obviously, the answers to these questions color our view of authority and obedience. The Church struggles to recognize the Holy Spirit's invitation to incorporate the influence of certain secular developments, yet also to recognize "limit" situations in which faith must firmly resist a secular spirit or development. Can the contemporary secular movement toward participative democratic decentralization finally lead us, as a Church, to bury any semblance of hierarchically centralized identity? This challenging question concerns one of those "limit" situations for our Catholic faith. If we are to face the issue honestly and carefully, we must avoid being trapped in the overly facile assumption that the governing style and organization of any group can only be hierarchically centralized or "participatively" decentralized. Felt membership in a local network or group will never suffice for full Catholic identity and mission. And one cannot help but wonder how much of the recent loss of a lively sense of felt membership, corporate identity, and missionary enthusiasm in certain church groups and dioceses has resulted from too much decentralization. The challenge facing the whole Church and every diocese is not to reject stubbornly every sign of participative democracy as corruptive and contradictory to Catholic hierarchical centralization. Rather, notwithstanding some of the strong secular influence of our American culture, the challenge is to devise a creative and appropriate way to integrate democratic decentralization and hierarchical centralization. This new, creatively integrated model could diminish an alienating sense of fragmentation and increase the sense of membership, involvement, and commitment to mission on the part of everyone in the Church or in a particular diocese. This article is an attempt to situate within such a creatively integrated diocesan model an understanding of the respectful obedience of diocesan priesthood.

Aspects of Obedience

A Christian disciple's experience of obedience is always religiously motivated. Johannes Metz, in *Followers of Christ*, pointedly describes the essence of Christian obedience: "Obedience as an evangelical virtue is the radical and uncalculated surrender of one's life to God the Father who raises up and liberates."[1] As a religious experience, obedience is a person's response to the attractiveness of God's love as revealed in the Spirit of Jesus Christ. Without enough genuine knowledge and love of Jesus, the life and service of obedience is quite deficient, if possible at all. Francis Moloney, in describing the evangelical imperative of obedience in *A Life of Promise*, claims that "Jesus did not found a group of disciples to *control* God's kingdom. He called them to 'follow' him, and to call others to pursue that same journey, to fall, out of control, into the hands of a loving and jealous God, as he leads them into *his* future."[2] And so, the disciple's obedience, however anguished or easy, is never a forfeiting of responsible freedom, even as it effects a union with God in love, deep peace, and energetic joy. Such a life of falling out of control into God is not a heroism of supererogation; rather, it "encompass[es] the whole of the Christian response" and makes obedience "certainly the most radically demanding of all the evangelical imperatives."[3] Once again, without a lively sense of God's love, the Christian life as obediently faithful response is hardly possible at all. Obedience, as all who practice and know it well, demands a spirituality that is profoundly rooted in such faith.

The Christian disciple's obedience to God's love in imitation of Jesus is also always ecclesial. It is mediated within and through the Church. Together with acknowledging the inviolability of an individual's maturely and competently formed conscience, it is important to recognize that the obedience of Christian discipleship is not simply an individualistic "God and me" encounter. Ecclesial mediation is central to the fundamental baptismal commitment and continues to play a central role in the obedience of other forms of consecration that further specify and develop that first foundational commitment. It is also the primary community and locus for the formation of conscience. And though Christian obedience is always finally oriented to an interpersonal experience of God's will of love, the Divine authority revealing this will of love is ecclesial and, therefore, is necessarily mediated in various human ways. When these channels of human mediation trouble and challenge us, as they often do, we cannot simply write them off as excessively legalistic minutiae or culturally outdated phenomena. Behind what seems to be simply an outdated governmental style or process of group dynamics may be something much more important: a profoundly theological, spiritual mystery revealed in Christ. And that is not disposed of too easily. The human channels of religious authority that mediate God's loving presence will always challenge us to find the proper contemporary expression, purified enough to symbolize honestly and simply in faith the Divine, loving source of all authority.

Because the obedience of Christian discipleship is always ecclesial and mediated, it happens within believers, is often encouraged by them, and deepens their corporate unity. When seen within the communal context, Christian obedience is, and cannot be other than, an interpersonal response to authority. Obedience and authority are so intimately related that it would be a serious mistake to consider the quality of priestly obedience as completely unaffected by the governmental style of local episcopal authority. This intimate interrelationship cuts both ways: a childishly unhealthy exercise of authority can invite an immature response of obedience; and only respectful, mature obedience invites a mature response from the bishop. The abandonment and submission of self involved in obedience cannot be oblivious to the style in which authority is exercised. A governing style that either allows others to do whatever they want or forces them to do something without any possibility of dialogue and understanding surely affects the quality of obedience. Even more importantly, such a governing style affects the unity and zeal of community.

Within the Christian community, the relationship of authority and obedience is not that of parent and child. Rather, it is the mature relationship of two or more adults in faith. Whenever a paternalistic or maternalistic interaction of parent and child is substituted for this relationship between peers, the interplay of obedience and authority is corrupted. An overly parental prejudice, especially when combined with a lack of much genuine experience of the expansiveness of God's love, can easily turn the radical entrusting of self in obedience into a whole range of authoritarian hang-ups. Precisely to avoid such authoritarian interferences, in recent years, many groups have changed a paternal and maternal imaging of the obedience and authority relationship to something more fraternal and sisterly—but sometimes without preserving the clear lines of religious authority and leadership.

Unity for Mission

This brief review of the fundamental mystery of Christian obedience as a religious, ecclesial, and adult experience in which one is always interpersonally related to authority provides a context in which the obedience of a diocesan presbyterate can be viewed as a corporate unity, energized for ministry. In contrast to the dynamic at work in a monastic group, this active vision and spirit draws apostles together for the sake of mission; coming together in community is not the chief and identifying characteristic of such a group. It is the desire to be sent forth that attracts the members to the group from the very beginning. And so, the unity of the group must never prevent the sending forth of the members; the group must find its fulfillment in precisely that missioning and dispersion.

As a result, although many other characteristics of the members may and should enrich the group's unity, the most profound and influential bond among the members is rooted in their appropriate sharing of the mission of Jesus. And the mission of Jesus is always rooted in the heart of the Trinity, in Jesus' full, intimate, shared life with His dear Father—that life of missionary love which is the Holy Spirit. In the passionate intensity of Jesus' presence and involvement in the world, we recognize the missionary love at the heart of the Trinity that sends Him forth. From far beyond the world, Jesus is sent; and He immerses Himself in the joy and sadness, the light and darkness, all the complicated entanglements of a fully human life. The mission of Jesus, therefore, is much more than the specific work He does. His mission cuts to the core of His being in an attitude and mentality always expressed in a distinctive context: compassion for His Father's urgent concern for loving justice in this world. It is this attitude, this mentality and presence, that lies behind and colors all He says and does and is. The gospel of John makes it especially clear that Jesus comes as one sent and that His mission is rooted in this continual, intimate experience of being sent by the Father. His mission is never a matter of sending Himself. There simply is nothing of auto-destination about Him:

because I did not speak on my own, but the Father who sent me commanded me what to say and speak. And I know that his commandment is eternal life. So what I say, I say as the Father told me. (Jn 12:49-50)

. . . I do nothing on my own, but I say only what the Father taught me. The one who sent me is with me. He has not left me alone, because I always do what is pleasing to him. (Jn 8:28-29)

It is to this missionary attitude and identity that the risen Jesus commissions His Apostles in the Upper Room: "As the Father has sent me, so I send you" (Jn 20:21). And the *Acts of the Apostles* bear stunning testimony to the corporate availability of the Apostles to be sent wherever the Spirit beckons. In fact, the corporate identity of the young Church seems to have consisted precisely in sharing this apostolic docility to the Word of God.

In the active spirituality of a diocesan presbyterate, both bishops and priests must approach the sharing of the mission of Jesus with an attitude that is similarly profound and, at the same time, as practical as the concrete process of apostolic placement. Insofar as an attitude of "being sent as Jesus was" genuinely motivates every member of the presbyterate, and insofar as this is incarnated in the placement process of the diocese, the priestly sharing in the mystery of Jesus' obedience—rather than simply resulting in individual ascetical experiences—can provide a corporate consciousness that will mission and unite not only the presbyterate itself but also the whole diocesan Church.

Radiating from the bishop to all the priests, this deep-hearted desire to be sent—something clearly contrary both to the trap of sending oneself and to an immature fear of making decisions—requires a humble self-confidence and continuing experience of God's missionary love in Jesus. The whole attitude and presence of the bishop, and the understanding of the diocesan placement process, must invite the prayerful initiative of each priest in an honest, unselfish investigation of God's apostolic will for him here and now. Sometimes, God's will is quickly manifested; at other times, it involves anguished soul-searching about selfish prejudices, profound contemplation of Jesus in His passion, and wide consultation with other people Throughout this initial stage and all the way to the end of the whole process, the individual priest—while very personally engaged—is never motivated by the attitude or expectation that his own decision about his ministry will be ultimate and self-assertively fixed.

Only a graced freedom can keep each priest seriously engaged in the placement process and ready to receive a ministerial assignment that is not simply his own decision. It is this same freedom that allows a priest's present experience of receiving a diocesan assignment to be a genuine sharing in the mission of Jesus. This freedom also prevents the same ministry's collapse into a defensively clutched attachment. The freedom needed here is not a passive lack of concern about a future assignment. Rather, it is a dynamic gift created by a strongly intimate experience of God's love and, therefore, a gift able to infuse an inspiration and energy without which God's apostolic desire might not even be recognized, much less embraced. When necessary, this freedom can even stretch the heart beyond the natural sensibleness of one's own mind to an agonizing self-abandonment to the precious glory of God, as corporately perceived and corporately served by a presbyterate gathered around its episcopal leader in the challenging, geographically specific range of the diocese.

Apostolic Placement Process

If the sending forth of active apostles is to deepen a unifying bond in Christ and avoid chaos and dissension, then the diocesan religious authority must employ a particular style of government and type of placement process. In this way, the apostolic availability and the obedient desire of each priest "to be sent as Jesus was" are invited and afforded concrete expression. Though various adaptations are possible, there must be a fundamental clarity of understanding about the placement process. Otherwise, what was never intended can happen: the process itself can confuse and prevent the desired corporate experience of obedience.

Part of this process is the expression of an overall apostolic vision and set of priorities in the diocese—not as unilaterally promulgated from on high but, in an appropriate way, as corporately determined within the whole body of the diocese. In this vision and set of priorities, the unity longed for on the part of the whole presbyterate takes preliminary expression, stirs the Spirit's apostolic inspiration in each priest, and provides a context within which each priest's serious opinion will finally be tested—and whether it is a genuine mission or not will be revealed.

Within a diocese, the role and lines of religious authority must be clear. If episcopal authority is truly to render a special service for the corporate unity of the whole diocese, then not only must its presence and role be similarly perceived by all, but it must also function in line with this understanding daily. In this view, each priest, through his prayerful engagement in the diocesan apostolic process, receives a specific ministerial assignment that has been decided interpersonally *with* him and intentionally *for* him but, finally, not simply *by* him. The bishop, who has himself been missioned in Christ, always has the final missioning authority in the diocese. This authority cannot be completely delegated to, much less usurped by, a personnel board or any other mechanism in diocesan structure. I do not mean to downplay the great aid that a personnel board or other diocesan structure can be to corporate unity and spirit. Rather, I want to repeat the point that the role and lines of religious authority in the diocese must remain personal, as well as clear, if they are to be directed toward unity of spirit and mission.

This view of missioning and obedience implies and requires a profound spirituality. Something more than sound organizational dynamics and conflict-resolution processes is needed. Often, in the absence of such spirituality, hidden agendas, political maneuvering, and various authoritarian hang-ups creep in and corrupt the experience of obedience. For the individual priest, "being sent as Jesus was" always culminates in an experience of receptivity and mature abandonment of one's whole self—a falling out of control of one's life and into God's providential love, as focused in the ultimate missioning decision of the bishop. Such an entrusting of self is hardly possible unless it is motivated by, and genuinely shares in, Jesus' own experience of the compelling attractiveness of a dear Father's faithful love. A profoundly incarnational faith is needed if one is to recognize and hearken to God's loving call, as mediated through the properly exercised episcopal authority of a specific, limited, and duly designated person. This human mediation, expressed in the person of the local ordinary and eventually grounded in a specific ecclesial understanding, is the quintessence of any incarnational view of diocesan priestly obedience. This mediation can also be the chief propellant toward a unified sense of mission within a diocese.

However, if a priest makes his own unilateral decision about a ministry, with whatever good will, or if he manipulates the accomplishment of his own will, even with the apparent legitimation of the placement process, he does not genuinely participate in or submit to another's decision. Instead, he "sends himself," which is quite opposed to the creative docility of obedience. This sending of self does not just segregate the individual; it splinters the corporate energy and zeal of the diocese.

The profound spirituality that inspires the diocesan placement process must include a genuine commitment to union in Christ on the part of the bishop and each of his brother priests. Without falling prey to a misguided, unrealistic sense of familial relationship or religious community, the seminary formation of diocesan priests must encourage a desire for, and some actual experience of, an appropriate corporate consciousness among the newly ordained. "Loner" and "rugged individualist" attitudes tend not only to disappoint the effectiveness of the individual priest's ministry but also to disrupt a unified diocesan experience of God's loving mission in Jesus. The clear, fresh air of honesty and trust must keep open all diocesan channels of communication.

A genuine concern for a sense of corporate membership and shared mission will make demands on the bishop and all the priests. It will take time and sacrifice and will test the creativity and commitment of all. Occasional, carefully planned gatherings of the whole presbyterate, priest support groups, shared silent retreat experiences of deep solitude, a diocesan newspaper, personal letters and phone calls, and many other means can create a corporate sense of priestly companionship and committed membership in the presbyterate. These are no luxuries for leisure time—joyous priestly celibacy demands such bonds of unity. And priestly obedience, when appropriately conceived and lived, can create such a corporate sense of unity and harness it with an enthusiasm for the generous service of God's loving justice within the diocese.

The Signs of Unity

The unity among the priests in a diocese is something much desired but often not sufficiently worked because of divergent expectations. Sometimes, the unity expected is too superficially uniform in terms of either type of ministry or geographical place. Ministerially, the unity of a diocese can depend too much on whether all the priests engage in the same sort of parochial work. Special, exceptional ministries may seem to interfere with presbyteral unity. Geographically, priestly unity in a diocese can depend too much on whether everyone serves within the limited are of the diocese. Although the call to serve a specific people within the boundaries of a diocese is central to diocesan priestly identity, the corporate solidarity of diocesan priesthood should run deeper than geography and should not seem disrupted by occasional (yet necessary) ministry outside the diocese. Although they surely have some effect on priestly unity, ministerial uniformity and geographical proximity cannot provide the deepest foundation for the corporate identity of a diocesan presbyterate.

The creative docility of priestly obedience, as expressed in the shared attitude of "being sent as Jesus was" through the proper diocesan apostolic placement process, can lay a much more profound foundation for unity and mission, rooted in the experience and heart of each priest in the presbyterate. Enthusiastic and unified service to all the people of a diocese demands much more than an uncertain unity superficially based on ministerial uniformity and geographical proximity. The people themselves expect more, and our promise before God of respect and obedience to the bishop makes us capable of a more profoundly corporate identity for mission.

This profoundly corporate and missionary identity of the diocesan priesthood can manifest itself in at least three ways. First, obedient unity in the experience of "being sent" produces a special consciousness of solidarity. Each priest knows that he has been missioned to a specific ministry in a specific place in order to share with his brother priests in Jesus' mission from His Father. It has not simply been a matter of his own choice. And so, to speak of administering a parish that "belongs to the whole diocese" is no cute or pious use of words; it delineates a clear mentality of corporate stewardship. Such an attitude, so different from the possessive one that clings to "my parish," conceives of every ministry as rooted in the Trinity and mediated through Jesus Christ and the bishop. When these become simply grandiose, high-sounding words, quite removed from the daily mentality and experience of the priests of a diocese, then they bespeak a serious failing in faith and defective priestly obedience. But if each priest's apostolic assignment is genuinely seen as rooted in the heart of the Trinity and mediated through Jesus Christ and episcopal authority and, therefore, somehow belonging to the presbyterate as a whole, then each priest will find his heart strengthened and encouraged by a corporate bond of solidarity and shared membership that stretches far beyond the physical presence of his brother priests. In the growing phenomenon of one-priest parishes, this encouraging bond of solidarity is nothing less than a lifeline.

Second, a corporate understanding of priestly obedience makes possible another important realization: that in some real way all the different diocesan ministries are of equal importance. Surely, in some ways, not all diocesan ministries are of completely equal importance. Yet if each ministerial assignment—from bishop's secretary to resident in the retired priest's home to pastor of a sprawling inter-city parish—is genuinely perceived and received as a particular brother priest's share in Jesus' mission in the Spirit from His Father, then there can be a basic and profound, if not total, equality to all these ministries. Far from an ethereal, vague distinction, this realization of the basic equality of all diocesan ministries is the best protection against some very real attitudes that we commonly adopt—especially competitive and ambitious attitudes that destroy diocesan unity. Whether one is assigned full time as prison, hospital, or military chaplain; whether one is pastor, assistant pastor, or simply in residence; whether one is assigned to an affluent suburban parish or to a financially insecure inner-city one; whether one receives a large or small salary—none of these circumstances will provoke ambitious jealousy and competitive rivalry if corporate priestly obedience reveals in some way the equal value of all diocesan assignments as genuine participations in Jesus' mission of being sent from His Father into a world so often darkly divided.

Third, the consciousness of priestly solidarity effected by shared obedience is also the best antidote, and perhaps the only effective one, to the kind of criticism that can divide a diocese—especially criticism of new and experimental ministries. If the few priests engaged in these new ministries know themselves, and are known by other priests of the diocese to have been chosen and sent as Jesus was, then in some real way, these special ministries belong to the whole diocese, to the whole presbyterate, and are not the possessions of the individual priests involved. Rather than disgruntled criticism or prideful possessiveness of these special ministries, what is needed is persevering support of prayer and priestly interest, especially since new and experimental ministries often involve unique loneliness and challenge.

Obedience Is a Shared Mystery

In this essay, I have presented a conceptualization—perhaps somewhat new—of the obedience of the diocesan priesthood, as promised before God to the bishop. I have described an apostolic placement process and governmental style that call forth and incarnate on the part of every priest in a diocese the shared mentality of being "sent as Jesus was." In this view, obedience within a diocese becomes much more than a set of traffic regulations or an empty protocol. Rather, as a profound mystery shared in faith, obedience becomes a life, a vision, and a mission binding priests and bishop together as servant members in the midst of the whole people united for evangelization.

I suspect that in some cases, any acceptance of this essay's suggestions may involve a challenging conversion of attitude and process—perhaps more than I can personally appreciate as a religious priest who does not live and serve within the ordinary diocesan framework. However, having developed a profound admiration and respect for the diocesan priesthood, I believe that we are well capable of, and could be deeply helped by, what I suggest here. Insofar as these suggestions become reality, I believe that the promise and practice of obedience will create a profound unity of priestly brotherhood—a brotherhood at once gathered around the bishop and decisively focused in joyful, magnanimous service to God's people.

All priests feel the need for the fellowship of priestly brotherhood, and wise ones seek it as best they can. We have learned in recent years, of course, that this can misfire into either an arrogant clericalism or an unhealthy "men's club" mentality. Or such bonding can be utterly nonexistent. But if we reconceive the implications of the promise of respect and obedience made on ordination day, then the fellowship of priestly brotherhood, besides involving enjoyable social times together, will be rooted in a shared religious experience of Calvary, where a faithful Son has fallen out of control into the loving hands of a dear Father—a Son who, then and now, in resurrection, knows and reveals a fullness of love promised for every diocese, its people, and its priests, whose hearts yearn profoundly for a new life.

NOTES

1. Johannes Metz, *Followers of Christ* (New York: Paulist, 1978), 67.
2. Francis Moloney, S.D.B., *A Life of Promise* (Wilmington, MD: Michael Glazier, Inc., 1984), 160-161.
3. Ibid., 119.

ABANDONMENT THAT ENLIVENS AND SETS FIRE FOR MISSION

In recent times, mission, community, authority, and obedience have not always blended well in religious congregations; but when a congregation carefully integrates these four elements, it possesses a healthy center of religious experience that makes possible a clarity of identity, a cohesiveness of membership, and most importantly, a fire for mission. The challenge facing religious today is not simply a matter of deploying members efficiently or satisfying ministerial preferences. Rather, the challenge includes a self-abandonment that renews the members' total reliance on a loving God while enlivening them and setting them on fire for mission, their hearts fused together in one consecration. The issue fundamentally is religious and spiritual.

Mission always has the overarching importance whenever it is related to community, authority, and obedience. Mission, as the very heart and meaning of any congregation, ties the members into the great desires of God as revealed in Jesus. Surely more than being just a job, mission draws its effectiveness from a spiritual theology, active and unitive within the hearts of all the members. At the same time, though mission has a priority over the three other elements, it can never replace any of them without seriously weakening the congregation's overall effectiveness and corrupting the significance of the element apparently replaced. Obedience when separated from the other three becomes an unhealthy ascetical practice, something shortsightedly in and for itself. Mission when separate from community produces a scatter-shot diffuse effect, and community without much relation to mission narcissistically turns upon itself. No, there is no avoiding the interrelationship of these four elements. The very identity and stability of a congregation depend on it.

A clear central integration of these four elements is as necessary for active as for monastic congregations, despite the significant differences between them. In religious life today, this fourfold central unity may express itself differently in the two, but it remains important for both.[1] Though not easily accomplished, this central unity can take on a critical importance in active congregations. Because it is the nature of an active community that its members be sent out and dispersed in a variety of ministries, the accomplishment of unity and a sense of felt membership can be difficult. But when the centrifugal force of ministry is not balanced with the appropriate centripetal force of community, the pain of disunity and loneliness can destroy the congregation. In many cases, the issue addressed here touches on nothing less than the very survival of the group.

Religious Life: Essentially Corporate Existence

Orders and congregations each have their own version of the evangelical imperatives of chastity, poverty, and obedience; but all of them have a corporate faith, focused in a shared vision and mission, that distinguishes religious life from other life-forms in the Church. In the midst of a great variety of changes within religious life, an essential corporate existence continues to play a central identifying role. And though the understanding of religious community has shifted a lot since Vatican Council II, only some clear shared corporate vision—believed and practiced by all—can prevent religious life from changing into a wholly different form. This fundamental communitarian existence stands as one identifying continuity stretching back event to Pachomius in the fourth century.

At a time of shifting meanings for religious community, care must be taken not to lose the reality. Especially in the active apostolic model, one of the revealing signs of a religious vocation continues to be a genuine desire for a shared faith and life. This must include some form of the following actions done together: sharing faith, praying, living, and ministering. These shared actions are not arbitrarily left to the individual's choice or whim. They constitute membership. So one is excused only for directly ministerial reasons. These commitment mechanisms ritualize in some genuine fashion the corporate vision and faith. Without such regularly shared experiences, the sense of religious community becomes ethereal and chimerical. Therefore, in some carefully understood sense, religious life *is* life in community, and not just on one's own. For an active religious, not to have a genuine desire to be together in praying, living, and ministering becomes a serious countersign to membership and cannot simply be tolerated.

This corporate shared life has within it a dynamic impulse to public, visible expression. The life-form of a secular institute runs on a different dynamic: to be hidden and unrecognized within the secular society. And so, ordinarily the religious life-form will stand out more than that of a secular institute. This element of public visibility gives external expression to the essential corporate nature of religious life. Of course, the evangelical imperatives, especially celibate chastity, add their own focus to this central corporate identity. My point here is simple and clear: religious life is not something done on one's own and alone. It is always a shared corporate vision and experience.

Mission: A Profound Spirituality and Theology

Mission is a great growing concern within religious life today, and well it should be. But this great concern can be misunderstood. In these days of second, third, and even fourth careers, more and more religious find themselves wondering, "What would I like to do now?" or "What should I try after ten years of teaching?" Though these and similar questions can naturally entertain our minds, they can fixate us on too superficial a level. As mentioned above, mission is not finally a matter of personal preference and efficient deployment of members.

Mission in religious life always catches fire in a profound theology and spirituality. Religious consecration gathers together and roots members in the mystery of Jesus' obedience to the great universal mission of God's love. A passionate desire for everybody to know how loved and cared for they are in the mystery of God is always burning in Jesus' heart. He is always on this mission. It is His very identity.

Jesus' consciousness is dominated by a sense of being sent. He never stands on His own. He never comes to do "His own thing." Whatever He speaks and does and is, He receives from another. The Gospel of John makes that point very clearly in many passages, such as: "I do nothing on my own, but I say only what the Father taught me. The one who sent me is with me. He has not left me alone, because I always do what is pleasing to him" (Jn 8:28-29). There is a clear limit to any process of self-actualization in Jesus. This clear limit does not speak of immature dependency, but rather points to a theology and spirituality of love always aflame in His heart.

The receptivity involved in Jesus' experience of mission reveals the central love affair that burns at the core of His identity. Rather than passive submission to the marching orders of some distant authority, mission for Jesus always radiates a life of love with the One He calls "my dear Father." At the heart of this love affair, a mysterious abandonment burns in an identity of perpetual adoration. It is an adoration that sets Him afire every day for His mission and finally, for the fearful but well-loved completion of that mission: the great Passover of His life. He does not tell His dear Father what to do. Rather, their self-abandonment in mutual love forges such a union that Jesus, aglow in the Holy Spirit, *is* God's mission always burning among us.

Jesus' Abandonment to His "Dear Father"

In this abandonment, Jesus' heart is always burning true. Sometimes, He shows His love by carrying out ordinary routines, while at other times, He performs deeds of high drama. All disciples of the great mission of God must do both kinds of things in their own lives, according to the specifics of their own personal religious experience.

In the temple at the age of twelve, Jesus speaks a word of truth: "Didn't you know that I must always be where my Dear

Father is?² This truth radiates identity for the young boy, as
well as for his distraught mother and foster father. While not
easily understood, such a word invites contemplative treasuring in their hearts. It not only cannot be contradicted, but it
alluringly presages a mysterious future.

Years later, this word has become so clear in His heart
as to call Him away from His beloved home and mother.
An urgency beckons Him, an urgency to go to His cousin,
the Baptizer, at the Jordan. There, the fire flames forth in an
enormously special way. A religious experience, always alive
in His heart, flashes forth in a dramatic moment. A love
beyond words and imagining; a Son so specially beloved and
pleasing; a servant uniquely chosen for mission—in such a
moment of abandonment of His life to His dear Father is
so very obvious and very right. He knows that this fire in
His heart has not been set by Himself, but by a dear Father's
loving Spirit. The original temple-word, now a clearly recognized relationship with a dear Father beyond limit, becomes
a guiding light all through His busy life in the midst of the
people. Always He is one called and sent in to the mission
of every day. This special inner consciousness keeps the fire
of loving abandonment zealously aglow in His heart. "I have
come to set the earth on fire, and how I wish it were already
blazing!" (Lk 12:49).

This inner fire burns finally into the completion of Jesus'
Baptism. "There is a baptism with which I must be baptized,
and how great is my anguish until it is accomplished!" (Lk
12:50). The growing paschal fulfillment of that temple-word
brings Him into the great missionary climax of His life. It is
high drama. A mission of love plays itself out on the stage
of His troubled heart, and the audience stretches into the

fullness of time. In an olive grove, His awareness that "everything is possible for you, dear Father" raises a puzzling possibility: "Take this cup away from me." But, beyond the fear and questioning of His mind, in the deepest adoring stillness of His heart, that fire of self-abandonment faithfully burns and enlivens: "But let it be as you, not I, would have it!"

This chosen servant, so much to the delight of God, brings the whole mission of His life to unending fullness in the climactic challenge of Calvary. Though the drama and intensity of the moment is high pitch, the story is still the same: a servant abandoning Himself to the Beloved. The mission of love is now somehow complete. "It is finished" (Jn 19:30). "Father, into your hands I commend my spirit" (Lk 23:46). Jesus, God's mission in our midst, stripped to the simple clear essence of His identity, becomes a fire of forgiving love blazing into the fullness of time.

Disciples: Sent for Mission

This enlivening fire for mission in Jesus is meant to determine the missionary lives of all His disciples. A great desire for mission and evangelization sends disciples all over the world. This evangelization must always be fueled by an urgency of desire that more and more people taste the joy, freedom, and union of God's deeply personal love in Jesus, a reconciling love in which we all live and move and have our being. Disciples always bring an astonishing wealth of gifts, training, and experience to this mission of evangelization. This is marvelous. The cooperation and blending of all these talents in any particular operation, however, is not always easy.

At the heart of this sense of mission must always be the same profound identifying attitude of Jesus. An eager, ready abandonment in love stokes the heart's coals for the fire of mission. Such missionary eagerness comes from a burning desire to be sent. This fire for mission involves a profound attitude in faith that becomes visible in the results of an appropriate ministerial placement process. Daily discipleship in the great mission of Jesus always requires the stance of radical abandonment that identifies Jesus in His love affair with His dear Father.

Various dangers today threaten the faith attitude and religious experience needed if we are to share Jesus' burning sense of mission. In recent years, many congregations have borrowed terminology from corporate management and social psychology to name roles played in the community's organization and structure.[3] While there surely is some value in this, we must be careful of the significance of our language. Language often has an effect on us that is not immediately evident. It can talk us into or out of certain attitudes, almost without our noticing. If we slip out of a profound faith perspective described in this article, a prophetic vision easily becomes ideological, and fire for mission becomes political competition. We must be careful that our words do not distract us from the realm of profound faith where the dynamics of life and love are often quite different from those of our secular society.

An age still strongly individualistic, therapeutic, and security-conscious keeps the focus on self and taking care of self. In ways insidiously subliminal, or at least not obvious, this spirit can lead to an assertiveness that resists the abandonment that sets a person afire for mission. Especially when this therapeutic spirit seems very convincing, the dynamic of "sending oneself" can quench the red-hot coals of missionary abandonment. Such self-sending is easily justified in the heady winds of assertiveness and individualism. Such self-sending often makes a person blind to any participation in the corporate vision; it blocks genuine community mediation and can even manipulate it. Such an attitude and practice threatens our sharing in Jesus' sense of mission. The issue finally is always the same: The self-abandonment that enlivens and sets the heart on fire is itself being abandoned.

An Abandonment to Whom?

The abandonment described here must be an interpersonal experience of love. Though we may pledge allegiance to a flag, we can abandon ourselves only to some person who loves us. Then, when the beauty of the beloved is magnetic enough, the abandonment becomes practically unavoidable. No mere cause, however noble and exciting, can affect us in this way, can move us as much as profound interpersonal love, engagement, and abandonment of self can.

The abandonment beyond self that participates in God's mission in Jesus always includes four loves or four ways of loving. *First* and foremost, we abandon ourselves into the loving hands of God. This falling out of control can never be forced or strongly willed on our own. We can only be lured and seduced to it by the astonishing beauty of God's love in the fidelity of Jesus. For someone who does not feel the magnetism of that love, the abandonment so central to this participation in God's mission not only will be almost unintelligible, but will also be altogether impossible. The person may even repel any such suggestion. The continuing struggle in active apostolic organizations to integrate mission and consecration is relevant here. A consecration to, with, and in God is necessary if mission endeavors—even fervently "prophetic" ones—are to become more than just efficient social work. In other words, the proper integration of consecration and mission can take place only in the actual experience of abandoning ourselves to God's love so radiantly inviting in Jesus.

Second, fire for mission also involves an abandonment in compassionate sensitivity to all sorts of needy people in our world. No impersonal cause, however rabidly espoused, will suffice. A specification and personalization of the great needs throughout our universe invites the missionary abandonment described in this article. For this aspect of abandonment to have strong effect today, certain countercultural developments are needed. Our hearts' desires and attentions must not focus on ourselves, but on needy people of the world. This calls for generous abandonment. The charism of each congregation must help its members to see needs in the world and then to set priorities in meeting those needs. The charism must be alive in their hearts so that they actually address some specific needs of today, rather than simply embrace a vague universalism. A charism that is trying to do everything runs the danger of accomplishing nothing.

Third, abandoning ourselves to a community of brothers or sisters who share the same religious consecration implies a belief that our corporate good is much more important than our own individual good. Community here must be not some idealized reality, but the real people of the here and now. This aspect of abandonment for mission does not make light of my own good, but presumes the pervasive corporate identity whereby my own sense of self cannot be conceived apart from the community's shared life and mission together. The central energizing concern is *we*, not *me*. Once again, corporate ministerial impact is what mission is about, not a scatter-shot effect of talented professional individuals. This corporate identity is not easily attained in an age of therapeutic individualism. It continues to be a major issue in religious formation today, and it must be resolved sufficiently at the time of profession if candidates and communities are to have a great future together.

Fourth, the abandonment we are discussing will always somehow involve human mediators who specify, clarify, and incarnate God's loving authority in Jesus for mission. Whether these mediators are friends, a spiritual director, a leadership team, a provincial, the bishop, or the other people with whom I live, mission can never be simply a matter of myself and God. The dialogue and discernment always assumes great importance, but is never the ultimate determining factor in the decision. In many situations, human mediation is precisely the point of struggle and disagreement among us. Some of this struggle is an understandable reaction of excessively authoritarian practices of mediation in the past, but not all of it is so easily explained. Some of this reaction needs to be explored and challenged. This brings us to the role of religious government in fostering a congregation's fire for mission.

Role of Religious Government for Mission

Models of religious government have gone through an enormous transformation since Vatican II. The diversity of development between men's and women's congregations has been striking. As we become sensitive to the enriching differences of the feminine and the masculine, the diversity of development is expected and is, perhaps, long overdue after many years in which women religious were forced into structures and models originally created for men. But some further questions surface at this point. Should the governmental models of congregations of women and men be *so* different? Along with some diversity that all seem happy to allow for, should there not be more similarity in the role of authority and the practice of obedience within men's and women's congregations? How do we recognize and maintain, both for women and men, a continuity of development with the past in this area of religious authority and obedience? (Such continuity, though not easily recognized at certain junctures in the development, is always a sign of the guidance of the Holy Spirit.) These questions are not easily answered. It is too easy a resolution to simply say: that is the masculine way and this is the feminine way. It is my hope that the diversity in this area between the practice of men and women will be mutually challenging and enriching.

A movement away from hierarchical models has characterized many congregational leadership arrangements since Vatican II. This movement was not so clearly called for in the Council's Decree on the Appropriate Renewal of the Religious Life, especially in its treatment of obedience.[4] Throughout all the documents of the Council, we can clearly find glimpses of a new vision for the people of God that would legitimize in the Spirit some of this movement away form a thoroughly hierarchical mode. But, without a doubt, other waves of influence gathering force over the last thirty years have been churned up and driven along by secular winds. Strong democratic and egalitarian presumptions have been hard at work deconstructing most models of authority and government. And, after tidal-wave proportions have been reached, it is hard to be concerned about nuance and degree of development and change. The Ignatian concept of authority and obedience for mission was strongly hierarchical and centralized. It was this strong centralized model of authority that made both internal cohesiveness and widespread external ministry possible. Some would view this Ignatian model as the beginning of active religious life in the modern world.[5] Congregations of women and men claiming Ignatian influence and roots in their founding interpret this in quite different ways today, however much they have, or have not, thought through and discussed the matter.

A triangular model of authority as flowing down from the pinnacle has given way to a model of much more mutual and shared responsibility. We are rediscovering the authority in each mature believing person. When well informed by the Holy Spirit and well in touch with God's people as a whole, each person is able to "author forth" as part of God's mission of love among us. But is this individualized, egalitarian authority enough for the mission of religious life in the future? If we simply let the recent decentralizing development have its way, will the proper understanding and practice of authority for mission just naturally emerge? I think not. Such a development implies too ethereal a view of the Holy Spirit, as though not inviting the cooperative hard work of human minds and hearts. Authority's triangle cannot be simply exchanged, in my opinion, for a circle composed of brothers and sisters of equal authority.

A Model of Concentric Circles

To properly integrate mission, community, authority, and obedience, I suggest another model for religious institutes:

concentric circles. In the centermost circle is God revealed in Jesus with a very special authority. In the next circle are the founders and foundresses with their charismatic vision and that vision's continuous development. In the next few circles would be individuals or teams on the general or local levels who possess an authority for unity and mission beyond that of all the other members. This special authority is received both from God and from all the members through the group's ecclesially approved process of choice. This distinctive authority does not finally set these people off from the rest of the members. As a matter of fact, it will have effect only as contextualized within the community of all the brothers and sisters. The people exercising such special authority are sisters and brothers to us all. This is precisely why these central circles are placed concentrically within the largest circle, which contains all the members gathered as brothers or sisters in one congregation.

In the concentric model, it is important to distinguish—but not separate—authority, leadership, and obedience.[6] Authority is a canonical, juridical office of power rooted in God, not in the chancery or some Vatican office. This is a power about other persons for ministry. Leadership, on the other hand, is a charism of influence and inspiration over other people. The latter cannot be legalized and institutionalized. Not everyone has this charism. Though the juridical office of authority and the personal charism of leadership can and should be distinguished, we must always work hard to keep the two in a proper balance of relationship. To give authority to someone utterly without the charism of leadership will usually not promote the corporate ministerial impact of a congregation. To confuse this distinction and the operative government model in a congregation will always have its corrupting effect on the unity of the membership and on its shared fire for mission. That lines of authority be clear regarding who exercises it and to what end is not a finicky concern for tidiness, but rather a strong desire for spreading fire effectively in the mission of God's love.

If authority and leadership must stay in relationship, the same is true of authority and obedience. They form an essential mutual relationship. One cannot stand without the other. While authority invites the mature obedience of careful listening, so too must it be sensitive in careful listening to the membership's calling forth healthy mature exercise of authority. Each calls for the other in a vitality and interrelationship always focused on greater unity and fire for mission.

The decentralizing trend in religious congregations since Vatican II has affected this interrelationship of authority, leadership, and obedience. It has, thereby, also affected the structure, appearance, and sense of belonging in many congregations. But as we keep relating this decentralization to two other corporate values (membership and ministry) and not allow it simply to develop a life of its own, a couple of important issues face us. How decentralized can a group become and still preserve a cohesive unity and an outreaching mission? How much unrefined pluralism can a group tolerate without losing its unity and identity? These questions not only nag at religious groups, but also affect secular organizations and are not susceptible to pat or easy answers. However, dealing with them is crucial because it keeps this decentralizing tendency in relationship with the foursome (mission, community, authority, and obedience) that provides the central stability and identity of any religious congregation. One of the dangers today is that this decentralizing spirit may assume a solitary dominating influence.

Religious authority, then, as exercised in the concentric government structure presented here, serves two major important purposes. In the first place, this authority fosters clarity and energy about the mission of God in Jesus for us here and now. Decisions are made, not simply according to individual preferences and serious individual discernments, but in light of a congregation's charismatic identity as that has developed over years to a contemporary specification. Authority, thus, exercises a preserving role regarding the congregation's present specification of its identity in the mission of God in Jesus. Rather than having a stifling effect, these mediators in the exercise of authority foster fire for mission and are servants of the faithful continuity of the congregation's charism. Of course, they could never serve this special role without the energetic cooperation of us all. In the second place, this authority is especially related to the corporate unity of the group. Just as God's authority is never meant to be an oppressing burden, but serves toward the uplifting unity of the whole human family, so this religious authority is a unique service for love in the unity and mission of the congregation. Mediators of this authority, therefore, are special servants of the group's unity in love. Without careful, clear exercise of authority and obedience, a congregation's experienced unity gets ragged, and its fire for mission dims.

Results of Healthy Integration

The proper interrelationship of mission, community, authority, and obedience produces four healthy results. First, ministry is always seen as rooted in and flowing out of the

Trinity. Neither empty theory nor impractical idealism, this profound spiritual theology must ground and animate all ministry in the Church. Ministry is really God's work and not some project that we are in sole charge of and that belongs completely to us. This vision of bedrock faith has very practical implications.

The second result is one of these practical implications. This Trinitarian vision of ministry keeps in check the serious danger of finding our very identity in the ministry. To succumb to the danger and identify ourselves in what we do is always to stunt the richness and profundity of our person. This is even more serious in terms of our identity in Christ. Whether consciously or unconsciously, letting our very identity—who we *are* in Christ—be consumed by our hands-on daily work has serious repercussions. Our view of self becomes superficial and overly pragmatic; we stubbornly cling for dear life to our ministry. The religious experience of taking genuine risks because of our reliance on God's promise in Jesus shrinks. Moreover, the physical decline of old age can bring deep frustration after many years of busy activity if we have allowed those years to teach us by osmosis this faulty maxim: *The harder we work, the holier we become.* As disciples called by Christ and saved in Christ, our identity is given; it is revealed, not earned, not merited. "For by grace you have been saved through faith, and this is not from you; it is the gift from God; it is not from works, so no one may boast." (Eph 2:8-9).

Jesus' Death on the Cross is our hope, our salvation. He is our identity beyond all others. In this greatest act of love, we find an identity so deeply rooted in God that we can be surprised: surprised by a ministerial availability beyond the limits we had mistakenly imposed, surprised by an experience of aging that invites an intimacy with Jesus beyond expectation. Once again, the central point of this article stands clear: Jesus' abandonment on the Cross attracts us and unites us in a similar abandonment that is the core of all ministry.

As a third result, when mission, community, authority, and obedience are meshing in the proper way, an invigorated sense of membership pervades the congregation. Members do not feel competitively alienated from one another in seeking, finding, and carrying out employment. Members, rather, feel part of a reality much bigger than themselves because their individual placement in ministry somehow really involves the entire community. Their daily ministry is part of the community's whole commitment to mission, extending far beyond individual preference into the enormous venture of God's mission of love in Jesus for the transformation of the whole universe.

As a fourth result, the proper implementation of the foursome described in this article enables a congregation to pool its resources, especially financial ones, and respond to some extremely critical contemporary needs even when the work is not recompensed by a living wage or any salary at all. A corporate commitment can overcome the limiting of ministries only to those that individual members find adequate to support themselves. In this way, availability for ministry is stretched beyond the limits of individual preference, individual job search, and individual income.

In conclusion, the Church throughout the world, especially in North America, faces the tremendous missionary challenge of a civil society becoming more secularistic, more permeated with a practical atheism. In the face of such a challenge, fear would distract our gaze and corrupt our courage. All the Church's members must respond courageously. But we religious, from the vantage point of our celibate, simple lifestyle, should be able to gaze and listen together in a specially sensitive and enlightened way, always eager for a self-abandonment that will enliven, not dehumanize, us and will set us on fire for mission beyond our individual likes and dislikes. The fire of this self-abandonment will constantly remind us that God is at the heart of it all and God's love in Jesus is the real work being done and to be done.

NOTES

1. See George Aschenbrenner, S.J., "Active and Monastic: Two Apostolic Lifestyles," *Review for Religious* 45.5 (September-October 1986): 653-668.

2. This is a translation of Luke 2:49 suggested by the Jesuit Scripture scholar Father David Stanley in a retreat given in 1967.

3. See Mary Linscott, S.N.D., "The Service of Religious Authority: Reflections on Government in the Revision of Constitutions," *Review for Religious* 42.2 (March-April 1983): 212-213.

4. Most commentators on the document notice an ambiguity within a variety of positions due to the conflicting views represented in the body of the Council and in the commission responsible for *Perfectae Caritatis*. See *Commentary on the Documents of the Vatican II*, vol. 2 (New York: Herder and Herder, 1968), 301-370.

5. See David Knowles, *From Pachomius to Ignatius* (Oxford: Clarendon, 1966), 61-68.

6. See Mary Linscott, S.N.D., "Leadership, Authority, and Religious Government," *Review for Religious* 52.2 (March-April 1993), 166-193.

PRESUMPTION FOR PERSEVERANCE AND PERMANENCE

Perseverance and permanence have never been easy for human beings, nor for cultures or civilizations.[1] These two conditions always require a commitment deeper and more courageous than that of passing fancy and temporary excitement. Yet, the dependability of persevering commitment is the very bedrock of any civilization. History reveals plenty of evidence that a gradual fraying of the bonds of permanency sounds a death knell before a full bursting of such bonds finally buries that culture or civilization.

In many ways, recent years have revealed a fragility, a difficulty, and a lack of trustworthiness in many basic personal commitments. A priest who has been ordained ten or fifteen years becomes bored and is tired of his commitment, so he begins to consider another lifestyle. A young priest falls in love, an experience that is healthy enough and not unexpected, but in the tidal wave of such emotion, quickly presumes that he has made a mistake in being ordained and seriously ponders leaving active ministry. These are just two examples of circumstances that have resulted in a rather large number of priests leaving their priestly commitment soon after ordination. Something is awry here.

What has happened in such situations? How do we explain such predicaments? Did the priest not really understand what he was promising? Is seminary preparation not realistic enough for today's world? Many other questions could be and usually are asked—and are often answered with a facile certainty. A full understanding is very difficult without careful investigation of specific cases.

I am not attempting a full explanation of such choices in this essay, nor, even more importantly, am I writing in judgment of men in such complicated and stressful situations. My undertaking is more modest. I will describe the intentional exercise of a specific practice that I am calling a presumption for perseverance and permanence. This concrete exercise occurs in the midst of a whole process of presumption of vocation that delineates and motivates the entire seminary program; it runs from seminary entrance until ordination, growing in seriousness and certainty as part of the future priest's preparation. I will describe the way this experience also prepares the priest for living a permanent commitment far beyond ordination, even until death.

Permanent Commitment in Contemporary Culture

No mature person expects permanent commitment to be easy, but for various reasons, its very possibility seems more questionable today than ever before. We have so canonized individual freedom as a supreme human value that responsibility to commitments is too quickly seen as an interference to our freedom. Growth in our appreciation of the developmental phases of human maturity has made us less sure of our ability to commit ourselves to being present and loving far into the future. Consider, after all, how radically and how often our identity shifts as we grow through these different stages (if we get through them at all!). More and more, people have become skeptical of their responsibility over the long haul and, so, are afraid to make promises that profess their deepest truth, especially in a way that involves a serious commitment of self over many years. From another perspective, contemporary culture has so enthroned autonomy and self-fulfillment that it is difficult to talk about commitments that can perdure beyond intensely self-absorbed feelings and projects.

Somewhere in all of this, a deep sense of self has either simply been lost or has become so superficially pliable as to seem almost infinitely changeable. Such belief in the radical changeability of self affects even the possibility of a permanent profession of this "self." In some cases, as in postmodernity, the permanent profession of a self is outright denied; in other cases, the denial is more subliminal but no less real. However this mistaken conclusion gets imprinted on us, the result is the same and bodes disaster for a correct understanding of the priesthood.

Original Presumption: Judgment of Acceptance into Seminary

The acceptance of someone into seminary preparation for priestly ordination must always be a serious decision based on enough preliminary hard evidence of a call and not just on whim or arbitrary intuition. A first judgment about the presence of the charism of diocesan priesthood forms the decision for acceptance of an applicant. Of course, the mystery of a vocation from God can never be completely reduced to a case of perfectly clear evidence. Though the mystery of a vocation is born and intimated in the clear evidence of

212 The Hidden Self Grown Strong in God

certain requisite attitudes, gifts, and genuine desire, such a
vocation ultimately transcends scientifically verifiable evidence. For this reason, a priestly vocation is never so immediately obvious as to bypass the years of serious preparation
needed to clarify, develop, and mature the call.

The presumption for priestly perseverance and permanence begins with entrance into the seminary and continues
to grow throughout one's life, even until death. The initial
presumption that begins seminary preparation is a judgment
shared by a number of related parties: the candidate himself,
the vocation director, the bishop, and the seminary staff. This
beginning presumption that opens the doors of the seminary
to the candidate must deepen over time so that a year or more
before diaconate ordination, it can be formalized in a way
to be described later in this essay. This presumption, which
is more and more personally assimilated by the candidate, is
finally validated by God through the Church at ordination.
After the Church's validation in ordination, the details of
priestly life and ministry are carefully discerned by using this
validated presumption as a rudder that provides direction and
balance in the swells and squalls of daily service.

In using the word *presumption*, I run the risk of being misunderstood. *Presumption* can seem as arbitrary as a figment of
someone's overactive imagination, as selfish as strong-willed
determination, or as misguided as a projection of someone's
unrealistic fancy. For this reason, I cannot stress enough that
what I mean by *presumption* here is a judgment based on the
evidence of hard facts honestly observed and interpreted. It
is a crystallization of grace, a moment of clarity that formal-
izes the quality of the candidate's loving relationship with
God in Jesus. As a caution against the misunderstandings just

mentioned, the presumption must be tested and reflected upon throughout the whole process of priestly preparation.

From the very beginning of seminary, this graced judgment of presumption invites a practical act of faith in the candidate's priestly vocation, first on the part of the candidate himself, then on the part of his spiritual director, his formation advisor, and the whole seminary staff. Serious selectivity of seminary candidates makes this practical faith both possible and importantly rooted in the known history of the man's vocation. At this early stage of presumption, the candidate is not very intensely concerned with permanence in his vocation. Still, certain important dynamics of discernment are called into play. Practical trust in one's vocation at this early stage means seeing God's hand in everything that endears such a life to the candidate, whereas anything, however reasonable, that disquiets the heart about such a life is not viewed as an inspiration from God. Living this initial presumption is really a continuation of the vocational discernment that led the candidate to apply to the seminary in the first place. A candidate's careful living of this early presumption can help him avoid the confusion of falling prey to emotional fluctuation that is always part of daily life. Such early basic vocational discernment makes these ordinary daily experiences instructive and reveals the Divine initiative, motivation, and perdurance of a priestly vocation.

A Later, More Mature Presumption

Years have passed since the presumption of a vocation that brought the candidate to the seminary. These years have not been spent completely in the enclosed world of the seminary; rather, they have involved encounters with many people in leisure and ministerial situations. Study, prayer, and other sharing with fellow seminarians have anchored the candidate's vocation beyond his own experience. His personal relationship with the Risen Jesus has also matured through regular prayer and solitude. Competent spiritual direction has helped the seminarian to read the signs of God's loving Spirit in the quiet of prayer and in the daily details and encounters of life, both when boringly ordinary and when intensely exciting. Such one-on-one spiritual direction has become the central structure in contemporary religious formation. It tailors the whole process of seminary to each candidate and helps him to adapt to and contribute to the present seminary community. In this way, the original presumption has been tested and deepened, or the candidate has already departed.

In the last few years of his training, the candidate becomes capable of a more serious and mature exercise of the presumption of his priestly vocation. At this time, much more so than at entry into the seminary, the candidate is capable of appreciating the permanence of priestly commitment. The development of awareness of, appreciation for, and readiness for permanence varies from candidate to candidate. Because of this, the timing of this expressed presumption cannot be legislated for everyone, whereas events such as the public profession of faith and request for Holy Orders can be scheduled and done together. This private exercise of presumption of God's call to the permanence of priestly commitment is the fruit of such a personally paced process of discernment that it prevents a group expression at some expected time. Though this exercise of presumption for permanence does have a strong corporate bonding dimension to it, as expressed here, it must fit the Holy Spirit's unique timetable for each individual.

Carefully Timed

The need for appropriate timing becomes clear as we further specify the content of this intentional exercise of presumption. Once again, beyond any sentimentalized wish or boyhood dream of priesthood, the content of the presumption of which I speak here is clear and definite. It is the presumption that God is calling a man to diocesan priestly commitment and ministry for the rest of his life, that God is calling a man to diocesan priestly identity until he dies. Of course, the whole identity of diocesan priesthood is included here, but the candidate now clearly and intentionally views the permanence and perpetuity of the commitment. As we will soon see, making such a presumption with genuine intentionality is instructive in some very important ways.

Such a presumption can be intended only after a certain maturation of the candidate's human and spiritual experiences. A fundamental human maturity in self-acceptance, self-actualization, and self-transcendence is needed if permanent commitment is to have any hope of perseverance; even more important, we are finally seduced to "forever" by God in an overwhelming experience of the eternal flame of Jesus' faithful love. This experience of this love does not necessarily register for the candidate as a subjectively peak experience, but its objective reality, when believed and assimilated, lures him away from tight, selfish control of his own life. It entices him to an intimate trust whereby he leaves the control and guidance of his life to the God of faithful love promised in Jesus. The permanence and perseverance I speak of here is never simply the result of human willpower but can, finally, only be motivated by and rooted in a radically religious experience.

If the candidate considers this further presumption before he is ready, he might be frightened and even overwhelmed by the prospect of perpetuity. From this perspective, permanence is usually viewed quantitatively: how many long years must I be faithful? A sign of readiness for such presumption is the developing realization that though the quantity of years *is* somehow involved, what is more important is a quality and depth of self-realization and of faith experience of God's love. Without such a developed awareness and capacity, an intentional presumption of permanence and perpetuity does not fit the candidate's experience—he is just not ready. The quality of his human and spiritual experience does not have the suppleness and tensile strength needed to hold firm under the weight of perpetuity.

Though this presumption of permanence cannot be made too early, backing it up too close to diaconate ordination also destroys its effectiveness. Ideally, the presumption spoken of here should be made at least a year or two before diaconate ordination. This timing is true for a very important reason. Such an intentional acceptance of God's presumption of permanent priestly vocation facilitates a final period of discerning that not only further clarifies God's call in the heart of the candidate but also gives him important lived experience of what his daily life will be from ordination until death. The mistake of attempting this presumption too early or too late is surpassed in seriousness only by one other possibility: not to have exercised such an intentional presumption at all before ordination. In this case, the candidate does not learn the important process of living discerningly in the light of a God-given identity and mission, a process that is meant to become the very inner structure of his life after ordination. The priest himself will feel this loss over time. Worst of all, the people to be served always suffer most from a lack of decisive and enthusiastic living of a permanent priestly commitment.

To make this presumption in the middle of theological studies is not some artificial "practice" of living like a priest. Were it to seem so unreal and artificial, this would be a sure sign that the candidate is not ready. No, the issue here is serious, and the stakes are high. The clear approval of the candidate in the external forum by the seminary rector and formation staff is expected as part of the process leading up to this special internal exercise of presumption. It is a serious moment of crystallized awareness in the candidate's relationship with Jesus the High Priest. This is no play-acting ruse. With the help of his spiritual director, the candidate recognizes not only his heart's readiness but, even more, its desire for such a special exercise of his relationship with God. He does not feel perfectly in control now of his priestly vocation; rather, the quality of his experiential lover relationship with the Risen Jesus is such that the candidate, aware of the high stakes, desires to rely on that love, whatever fear may be quaking in his heart at the prospect of such fidelity.

The actual performance of this presumptive act before God is a private matter between the candidate and Jesus. It should be planned in stages so as to express its importance and significance in an intimately personal way. Whether it is done after the great central act of communion at Eucharist or in quiet prayer in a candlelit room, it is a moment to be ritualized and journaled with great care. It is a day that stands out in the ordinary events of life, a special touchstone along the journey to priesthood, an experience to be revisited often and meant to provide guidance long into the future. The candidate's heart has settled on a rudder for balance, a compass for direction that has never been so intentionally acknowledged before. The precise point of this presumption is permanence and perseverance of joyful service in diocesan priestly commitment.

Final Stage of Preparatory Discernment

This exercise of presumption of priestly permanence made in the middle of theological studies brings into focus an important final stage of discernment of priestly vocation. Discernment is the interpretation of all of our interior life, especially its spontaneous dimension, according to an acknowledged, profound identity in Jesus. Before this acknowledgement of profound Christian identity, trustworthy discernment in sifting through and interpreting interior experiences is not possible. The process of developing a more refined discernment as we clarify and deepen our identity in Christ is gradual for us all. The candidate's life now, especially until ordination, is a matter of prayerfully sorting through daily experiences in presumption of permanent priestly identity and ministry.

This presumption of priestly permanence till death has implications that the candidate must be courageous enough to recognize and live. The rudder of such presumptive priestly identity provides guidance in interpretation that gives clear direction to life. In an even more important way, this daily interpretation deepens priestly intimacy with Jesus and insures faithful presence and service in the midst of the people. This presumptive stand for priestly fidelity reveals the consoling synchronicity of some inner experiences as the continuing call of God which, when followed, will deepen priestly identity. The same presumptive stand reveals the desolate dissonance of other inner experiences as the disquieting influence of an unholy spirit deceptively leading one away from God's priestly call. When these latter experiences are honestly interpreted and courageously resisted, the candidate's priestly identity, once again, deepens.

Presumably, the major part of the candidate's busy daily life will reveal the consoling consistency of his inner life with his priestly vocation. His desire for and satisfaction with such a life and ministry will expand and refine his heart. Vocational temptation cannot be absolutely avoided, however. It is an important dimension of the development of any person's vocation in Christ and is rooted in the divided nature of human consciousness and of all reality. The candidate, at times, will find his feelings tugging—perhaps even straining—against his priestly presumption. In this way, his priestly vocation and identity are being tested and purified. Honest interpretation and courageous resistance will help him to believe in God's call beyond what he is now feeling. Without the rudder or compass of his personalized presumption for priestly permanence, such interpretation is much less sure, if possible at all. A man can easily fall prey to the swells and shifts of inner mood and emotions and, thereby, lose his balance, whereas a well-recognized and personally grasped norm can prevent a fundamental feeling of defenselessness. His intentional self-identification in the presumption for priestly permanence can keep him upright in the buffeting of life's stormy seasons.

As mentioned earlier, discerning from such a priestly presumption is very instructive for the candidate in this last stage of preparation before ordination. To have experienced the fittingness of this priestly presumption in the course of his development over the years will reveal, in the majority of cases, an even greater clarity and humble confidence about his priestly call. Such a candidate clearly recognizes this readiness and confidently requests acceptance for ordination. This readiness has been facilitated by spiritual direction, by the whole formation process, and especially by his practice of this final priestly presumption. Much less risk accompanies a petition for orders when the candidate is aware of, and relishes, the "feel" of the permanence of priestly commitment.

On the other hand, this intentional presumption can also force the issue of a lack of basic peace and contentment in the priestly call. An ongoing onslaught of inner experiences against priestly commitment prevents the basic joy and contentment needed for lifelong priestly service. In this case, honest interpretation and courageous resistance, as a matter of fact, do not buttress the priestly presumption made. What the candidate may have wanted in some vague but untested way now proves not to hold. What I speak of here is not just one crisis or another but a pattern of discontent over the remaining years before ordination. Usually, signs of such discontent have also appeared previously. In cases such as this, the intentional presumption of priestly permanence has crystallized the awareness that God is not calling this man to perpetual diocesan commitment. Such a person leaves the seminary with a clarity and peace that allow him to follow wherever God is now leading. This clarity is a more welcome blessing before ordination than after.

Ordination: The Presumption Ecclesiastically Ratified

Seminary preparation is not simply directed toward the exciting event of ordination but rather, toward the lifelong identity and ministry of priesthood. Though priestly ordination as an event of self-congratulation can, at times, disturbingly assume too selfish an importance and, thus, distract from the whole identity and ministry of priestly service, nonetheless, the petition for and conferral of orders is obviously a major step in the journey of seminary preparation. As described already, the whole process of presumption of permanent priestly vocation brings the candidate to a humble, confident, and informed petition for ordination to the priesthood. This petition is sanctioned by the seminary staff, led by its rector, and ratified by the approving applause of the local people from whom the candidate has been chosen. The whole process of seminary formation, aided by internal and external forums in their own distinctive ways and dramatized in the lived presumption of diocesan priestly permanence, finally brings the man to approval for ordination.

The Rite of Priestly Ordination is an act of God in and through the Church. In this way, the candidate's presumption of priestly vocation and perseverance, which has grown throughout his seminary years, is now validated publicly in the Church. Obviously, this action is never done impulsively or without careful consideration of compelling evidence. It is an action rich in revelation: for God, revealed as gloriously transforming Love; for this local presbyterate, in its special role of revealing that Love; for the new priest himself, now empowered to be a special priestly enfleshment of that Love; and finally, for the people, served in invitation to their own unique radiating of God's glorious love in Jesus. This day, deserving full and grand celebration throughout the whole Church, should also imprint itself deeply on the heart of the newly ordained. A whole future life of faithful ministry is powerfully poised in this event.

This ecclesial ratification of the presumption of God's call to permanent priestly identity and ministry gives assurance and encouraging clarification for the rest of the new priest's life. This assimilated presumption, though very helpful for the new priest, is not enough just by itself to get him through the transition of the first few years. Gatherings of new priests sponsored by the presbyterate, the mentoring help of a senior priest, and the honest encouragement of parishioners are meant to complement the new priest's personal preparation. The priest's presumption is now even more public than when done in the seminary and is not just some private devotion between himself and Jesus. As publicly ratified in the Church, it has a certitude and clarity that can stay with the priest through the rest of his ministry. This presumption, tested and ever more personally assimilated over the years, now stands as a rudder, a compass, a beacon giving light, balance, and direction for the future. The last few years of training have especially fit this rudder to the "feel" of the new priest's heart. His gaze has been focused on that beacon, and he has learned to read that compass.

Now, his priestly life with all its rich and exciting variety will be enlightened in the daily presumption of permanent priestly ordination. The discernment experienced previously in line with his presumption of priestly permanence is an invaluable aid in his daily life. Whatever in his interior life further reveals and deepens his priestly identity is presumed to be of God's Holy Spirit, whether it involves obvious joy and satisfaction or invites him to a painful, difficult challenge. Whatever deceptively interferes with his priestly call, whether a mood of happy feelings or a burdensome feeling of boredom and failure, is now interpreted as the temptation of an unholy spirit. Following the guidance of God's Spirit in resisting the deceptive insinuations of the evil spirit becomes very practical and concrete. Insightful courage and trust in God's promise of a faithful priestly call become the issue at hand. Now, the young priest who falls in love presumes that this is not a call away from priestly commitment. Rather, the issue is what kind of relationship, if any, he is to welcome with this woman. The priest who is bored and losing the glow of his priestly commitment presumes he is not being called away from priestly ministry but must, rather, investigate means to renew himself and rekindle the fire of his permanent priestly identity. This presumption of priestly permanence is paramount in the new priest's heart and provides vocational interpretation in every situation. He has learned this over years of growth into intentional identification with this presumption of priestly permanence.

This identification of self with presumptive priestly perseverance is not an exercise of the superego or some Kantian moral imperative. As mentioned earlier, this presumption is rooted in an ever-developing experience of God's intimate, enlightening love in Jesus. This experience of the fire of love in Jesus' heart that rooted and revealed the man's priestly vocation in the first place must continue to grow in the intimacy of prayer and discernment. Otherwise, the ratified priestly presumption of permanence will lose its radiance. No superego empowers the priestly presumption. It is the continuing ignition and flame of a love affair with God in the beauty of Jesus the High Priest. This priestly presumption is not to be clung to irrationally or blindly; rather, there is the clarity and power of vocational commitment radiating from a love that will stake all in relying on the Beloved's promise to be faithful and to guide us always.

Conclusion

The presumption of priestly permanence presented here should play a central role in seminary preparation. If the candidate does learn such a presumption, it will make a difference in his preparation for petition for priestly ordination. It will also aid him in the joys and trials of priestly ministry.

What I am speaking of is no magic wand with which a priest waves his way through his ministry or some unbreakable walking stick clung to for dear life. The presumption this essay has described is meant to become the inner structure of the priestly candidate's heart, a heart becoming more and more inflamed in God's attractive love as revealed in Jesus. This inner drive of love, enlightened and eager to be faithful to God's glorious dream for the whole universe, always finds focus for a diocesan priest in fidelity to a particular local people. This presumed fidelity requires the courage to stand firm in a promise and profession unto death, just as Jesus did, especially on Calvary, where the light and hope of Resurrection originally dawned slowly and now burns with a permanent radiance.

NOTES

1.   In this essay, I have slightly revised, with permission, what was previously published as "Presumption for Perseverance and Permanence: Rudder for Direction and Balance in Priestly Formation," *Seminary Journal* (Spring 1988).

A Celibate's Relationship
with God

I affirm the vocation and value of religious celibacy, not as something easy that requires no sacrifice, but as something demanding that is full of joy and love and energized by God through religious community and ministry. It is a way of living that can be spiritually challenging and psychologically healthy. The adventure of a healthy celibate life is always the integration of its sexual challenge with a profoundly intimate and lively spiritual life. My central focus here, however, is not the sexual dimension of celibacy but the delicate and decisive balance that religious celibacy must achieve between the following three essential relationships: a distinctive companionship with God, a life and faith shared in religious community, and a ministry shared with many other people.

Toward a Descriptive Definition

As a mystery of faith whereby God attracts men and women to a particular experience and style of life, celibacy defies any final scientific definition; in fact, it is impossible to begin to comprehend celibacy without faith. Karl Rahner, in *Servants of the Lord*, calls it "part of a theology on its knees, at prayer."[1] He further observes that "it is odd how we always speak of celibacy in general . . . To take refuge in generalities about such a subject is misguided, dangerous, and self-defeating . . . You and I must ultimately ask not 'What of celibacy *in itself?*' but 'Where does my celibacy stand?'"[2]

The simplest view of celibacy is the one held by many ordinary people with little theological, spiritual, or canonical sophistication: that celibacy is a matter of not having a husband or a wife. Though this view is somewhat superficial and negative, there is obviously truth in it. It would, however, be more precise to say that celibacy is the foregoing of all genital sexual expression in the basic threefold sexual relationship we all have with ourselves, with members of the same sex, and with members of the opposite sex. But defining religious celibacy as the negation of specific external actions is unsatisfying and fails to catch its attraction and power. Nonetheless, even this early, superficial stage of definition can provoke some interesting questions and insights. Some would claim that renouncing children is a greater sacrifice for women than for men. A woman religious who is a friend of mine believes this to be so, and wonders whether much of this sacrificial value is now being lost on young women who, unduly influenced by our culture's stress on self-protective comfort, do not have the raising of a family as a serious goal. If the object of the sacrifice is not strongly desired, the cost and value of the sacrifice decrease.

Attitude Toward Reality

We may now take our initial definition a step farther and describe celibacy as the choice not to have a marital partner. In its more profound sense, beyond the renunciation of any specific man or woman as a husband or wife, this choice implies an attitude of special presence and relationship to all reality, in which one relates to nobody and to nothing as one would to a husband or wife. Keith Clark, in *An Experience of Celibacy*, explains that the celibate does not belong to, nor is owned by, anybody or anything as husbands and wives belong to and own one another in the beautiful intimacy of Christian marriage.[3]

On a more positive note, we can talk of celibacy as the experience of discovering one's heart to be, in the words of Peter van Breeman, "unmarriageable for God's sake."[4] This brings us much closer to the heart of the matter. To be unmarriageable here is not seen as a curse or a failure. In fact, a human being must first grow to a mature sense of responsibility and marriageability before the realization gradually dawns that he or she is actually becoming unmarriageable. Van Breeman puts it well in *Called by Name*: "Celibacy does not mean that one has lost something, but rather that the celibate has found Someone."[5]

Celibacy, therefore, is the only fitting human response to a specific kind of companionship offered by God. As the religious experience of men and women develops a distinctive quality of intimacy and attractive aliveness, they feel themselves seduced into such an abandonment to this companionship with a dearly loving God that they cannot also take upon themselves the abandonment and union involved in a marital relationship with another human being. In and through all the loves in their lives, they have come upon a Love that transcends and surpasses all others, and they sense their hearts expanding and filling with that Love. This is not to claim that the experience of God found in celibacy is better, more thorough, more intimate, or more holy than that found in marriage, but rather that the celibate person's experience of God is different in contour and destiny from that of the married person. So understood, celibacy is rooted in a person's religious experience of the awesome attractiveness and thorough invitation of God's love.

A Foundation That Takes Years

This kind of religious experience does not suddenly erupt; it develops over years. Formation personnel must learn to recognize the signs of this development that are requisite for first commitment and those that are requisite for final profession years later. Along the course of this development, there will be privileged moments of insight into and recognition of the celibate companionship and vocation that are being offered. Only through prayerful discernment and careful experimentation with commitment to the vocation revealed in such an experience of God can one's heart finally come to the inner confirming explanation: I can do no other!

Only a distinctive religious experience of God can lay a foundation that will be profound and permanent enough for the life of religious celibacy. Any attempt to justify or explain this celibacy simply in terms either of a shared life and faith or of a response to the sorry state of our world today is doomed to failure. The soundings for celibate identity must run so clear and deep as to touch the very being and love of God. Though there are always many factors contributing to the growth of a vocation, only the infinite beauty of God, who is more in love with us than we are with ourselves, can fascinate a human heart to celibacy. When candidates for a celibate vocation say that they are motivated by a desire to serve this world and its people, formation personnel must

help them to find, behind and beyond this valuable motivation, the distinctive quality of religious experience that gradually becomes a clear call to a celibate relationship with God.

Honest, prayerful reflection is more necessary for the
development of a celibate vocation than superhuman psychic
strength. I have been involved more than once in a discussion about whether celibacy demands a greater inner psychic
strength than married life does. Obviously, the psychological
vigor that results from healthy self-acceptance and self-love
is needed for all happy, mature celibate living. But since this
vigor is needed for any mature human life, it is a mistake to
make a simple equation between a vocation to celibacy and
greater inner strength. A truer way of discovering a celibate
vocation is to reflect seriously and prayerfully on the whole
range of one's social relationships. This variety of experience
of love, intimacy, and other human sharings will inevitably
lead certain people away from focusing on a future marital
relationship and set their hearts' sights on God's love in the
growing desire to be owned by that love alone. In the end, it
is the distinctive companionship with God alone that makes
celibacy genuinely religious and adds to a celibate lifestyle the
possibility of fidelity.

A Threefold Relationship

By synthesizing many of the insights already mentioned
and adding a new and very important perspective, we may
arrive at a final definition of religious celibacy as the human
presence of someone who lives without a marital partner in
response to God's invitation to a distinctive companionship
that is shared in religious community and helps to further the
Kingdom of Jesus' Father in human hearts. This definition

needs further explication. Celibacy is not simply a negation, nor the performance of certain external actions, nor an inner attitude, nor a private, religious experience; rather, it is a specific human presence in the world. This presence is only possible as the result of an essential threefold relationship that comprises a relationship of distinctive companionship in faith with God, a relationship of shared life and faith in religious community, and a relationship in ministry with many other people. It is not possible to choose only one or two of these relationships; all three are required and offered in a celibate vocation.

Although these relationships are all necessary to the contemporary understanding and living of celibacy, there is a clear hierarchy of importance. Celibate identity must strike deeper than the necessary involvement in religious community and in ministry. It must reach to the very heart of an experience of God in a special companionship. To upset this primacy, to try to sink the roots of celibate identity primarily in community or in ministry, can lead to serious misunderstandings.

We have long been familiar with these three relationships, but we have not always recognized or honored their interdependence, which I believe is crucial for happy celibate living. In daily living, celibacy has often been interpreted simply as a special relationship with God. Whenever some problem with celibacy arose, in the end, the solution was always to pray more and relate better to God. But when celibacy is viewed in terms of a threefold essential relationship, it is clear that some problems must be solved by readjusting our community or ministerial involvement, not our involvement with God in prayer. Let there be no misunderstanding: a profoundly personal involvement with God in prayer is absolutely critical for effective celibate living. But such a prayer relationship with God, essential as it is, is not enough. Whether the life of a celibate will be characterized by frustrating tension and strain or peaceful energy and intensity depends upon the carefully discerned integration and balance of these three relationships. This integration does not come automatically and completely with prayer; it must also be sought in human relationships, both in community and in ministry. Nor is this integration something static that can be preserved everlastingly, once found. Rather, it is a dynamic reality that shifts and develops from phase to phase of a person's life. Thus, the challenge for the adult celibate is to find and live the proper integration that will balance the potential tension of these three relationships with an energetic peace and enthusiastic joy.

Relationship with God

The most important aspect of this essential threefold relationship is that distinctive companionship initiated by the mysterious workings of God's love in a person's heart, to which, finally, the only appropriate response is a celibate lifestyle and presence. A profoundly personal and intimate solitude, a standing alone in and with God, is at the very heart of celibate existence. This aloneness with God is always a gift; it can never be the result of human effort. It is, however, a gift that the celibate must learn to receive and cooperate with. At times, this aloneness calms and focuses one's center of consciousness and expands one's heart in intimacy; at other times, it is a loneliness that shrivels the heart and rattles the bones. Nevertheless, in faith, it is always a power to transform

234 Hidden Self Grown Strong in God

234 *The Hidden Self Grown Strong in God*

and poise a heart in self-oblative love toward the Other and all the others.

Modern American culture, in many ways, militates against the experience of aloneness. Without denying the need for supportive friendships of all sorts, the celibate does, in some sense, stand alone in this world. The companionship in which this aloneness is rooted is lived in the darkness of faith and the enthusiasm of hope; there is no kind hand to hold, no eyes to gaze into, no lips to kiss. But it is a compassionate companionship of such intimacy in faith that it can promise the human heart more than anything else in this world ever could: fulfillment of our deepest and truest longings. The profound faith and patient hope required for such celibate companionship with and in God will always be challenged, even ridiculed, by an exaggerated stress on the importance of sensual feeling. To stand alone seems freakish in a culture obsessed with the sensual and the sexual. Celibate existence will always be countercultural in the face of such an immature attitude, and it will seem just as countercultural in any church or religious group influenced by this attitude. Nevertheless, though it is true that infatuation with sensual feelings can distract one from the call to profound faith, celibates are not bound to scorn and flee the sensual but rather are invited to discover, develop, and live their sensuality in an appropriate way in relationships with God and with many other people.

This aloneness of celibate existence with and in God is a necessary witness to the whole human family, for it symbolizes something fundamental to the human condition. Henri Nouwen has referred to celibacy as "an emptiness for God."[6] At the center of every human heart there is a space, an emptiness, available to no one besides that unique human being and the God whose love is creatively holding that person in being. This emptiness is truly for God. To gradually discover, accept, and live out of this center is the maturity of human and spiritual identity. Some men and women, as they experience this core celibacy more fully in their hearts, hear a call to express it in a lifestyle of religious celibacy within the Church. Detached from the core celibacy, this lifestyle would become superficial, showy, and rootless. It is for this reason that Nouwen maintains, in *Clowning in Rome*, that "we will never fully understand what it means to be celibate unless we recognize that celibacy is, first of all, an element and even as essential element in the life of all Christians."[7] The celibate lifestyle reminds all of us that the human heart by its nature contains an emptiness that invites solitude. Celibacy stakes a claim in the heart at a depth that is available only to our creatively loving God. "Thus," says Nouwen, "in a world torn by loneliness and conflict and trying so hard to create better human relationships, celibacy is a very important witness. It encourages us to create space for him who sent his son, thus revealing to use that we can only love each other because he has loved us first."[8]

The affective renunciation of the possibility of having a husband or wife, when properly understood, enhances the meaning and witness of celibacy as a unique relationship with God. But this renunciation must be something much more than a mere negation, for a simple denial could never be sufficient motivation for the human heart. The renunciation must cut deeply enough to amount to a re-annunciation of the celibate person's whole identity. Celibates proclaim their core identity to be thoroughly and carefully centered in God. Celibate disengagement from a spouse announces a profound and intimate engagement in faith with the awesome mystery of a loving God.

Disengagement Becomes Creative

The disengagement that I am speaking of reflects the Calvary disengagement of Jesus, which was a deathly disengagement for life—difficult, yet freely chosen in such a way as to witness unequivocally to His lively and thorough engagement with the One He called "My dear Father." And His Father blessed that disengagement with a fullness of life and love in resurrection. As Sandra Schneiders has persuasively argued in the journal *Sisters Today*, the death disengagement of Jesus and of the celibate is creative—creative of a Kingdom fullness, to be looked for in hope now, and to be lived in joy finally.[9] Thus, celibate disengagement not only bespeaks a special engagement with God on the part of the celibate person, but also announces to all Christians that their identity, however necessarily and intricately involved it is with this world, finally is not of this world, but is fulfilled in that fascinating and mysterious Father of Jesus whose Spirit throbs in all our hearts. As Schneiders points out, however, celibacy can be creative only if "such a disengagement, such an engagement with God . . . is completely, authentically, generously, and unselfconsciously lived."[10]

Most authentic, unselfconscious living of celibacy is born of responsible dealing with loneliness. The uniqueness of each person makes loneliness an inescapable part of the human condition. Celibacy, because of its disengagement and affective renunciation (surely, never meant to be a renunciation of all affectivity!), often brings in its wake a distinctive type of emptiness and loneliness with great potential for fostering the development of a mature self-possession and a richly intimate life with self, with others, and with God. If this loneliness is not properly controlled, however, it tends to fragment us, leaving us with an anguished sense of alienation from everyone, and becoming a desolation destructive of our relationship with our true self, with others, and with God.

On the other hand, when celibate loneliness is faced and dealt with, it becomes productive and enriching. Though there are similarities between biting loneliness and confident aloneness, the differences between the two outweigh the similarities. Instead of being "fragmenting," aloneness, as the word itself suggests, has the sense of being "all one." It is the centered wholeness of humble self-possession carefully poised for service. Unless people spend enough time alone, it is hard for them to be really at home with themselves, to have that basic comfort with themselves that makes possible true maturity and responsible generosity.

Solitude Centers Existence

Recognizing both the distinction and the relationship between loneliness and aloneness is an important aid to living a celibate identity. It is precisely the affective renunciation of marriage and the careful dealing with the resulting emptiness that make possible an even deeper development of that con-templative solitude all alone with and in God—the center of celibate existence. But this productive dealing with loneliness is more easily described than accomplished. Instead of suf-focating in the clutches of loneliness or repressively denying its existence, we must learn to be present in the loneliness in such a way as to be able to recognize within the emptiness a call to renew our celibate identity in the intimacy of solitude, alone with God as the Beloved of our heart. To face the loneliness, to accept it as part of life, and yet to avoid being mastered by it by transforming it into a renewal of celibate identity usually involves the use of specific practical tactics that are as varied as the people who make use of them: a wrestled act of adoration in the flickering darkness of a chapel, the exuberant exhaustion of physical exercise and hard work, the pleasant enjoyment of music and reading, or the heavenly delight of time with a friend. There are many other possible tactics, but in all the variety, the choice and the motivation are the same: to decide against the destructive loneliness, by hearing within its depth the renewed invitation to find one's truest self, with all one's power poised for service, alone in God's love. This ability to deal with loneliness so as to transform it into celibate solitude in God is obviously an important sign of a celibate vocation during the early stages of religious formation.

For Composure of Consciousness

A celibate vocation should also involve the development of a genuine theology and spirituality of "my room" and "my bed." This is quite different from the marital theology and spirituality of "our room" and "our bed." Most men and women do not usually sit alone in their room or go off to be alone. The celibate, however, retires alone at night and arises alone in the morning, and during waking hours spends a great deal of time alone in a room, either preparing for or debriefing ministry. It is often in the celibate's own room where nagging loneliness can tempt the soul and sap enthusiasm. A theology and spirituality of "my room and bed" must be realistic enough not to delude the celibate into thinking that future loneliness can be prevented, and it must be profound enough to help the celibate transform this ordinary loneliness into a contemplatively relaxed and intimate solitude with God in love. To be profound and realistic, such a theology and spirituality must be manifested in this world—even in things as seemingly minor as the arrangement of one's room. Of course, something as personal as the décor of one's room will vary from individual to individual; yet, when it succeeds, it will help one to find a composure of consciousness focused not on self but on the fascinating beauty of God experienced here in one's room as the Beloved of one's celibate heart. In so describing one's room, I do not mean that it should be a fortress to protect the celibate from community or a place for selfish indulgence. It need not even be the space within four walls and floor and ceiling. A theology and spirituality of "my room" and "my bed" can also be developed when one is forced by circumstances to share a room with others because, finally, it is a composure of consciousness that focuses the affectivity of one's heart so thoroughly in the intimacy of God's love that one is poised in freedom for service and relationship with anyone anywhere.

Obviously, this kind of theology and spirituality is not automatically acquired; it must be intentionally developed through hard work over years. If it has not been developed, then celibate living will be more haphazard and less joyous and intimate than it could be, both with God and with others. Certainly, part of the hard work involved in forming the theology and spirituality of "my room" and "my bed" is the faithful practice of daily contemplation. Without it, a human heart cannot know, and surely cannot persist in, the developing and distinctive companionship with God that I have described here as the very heart of a vocation to religious celibacy. Without this enduring contemplative involvement with God, it is hard to see how a person's celibate relationship with God can energize him or her for selflessly free and lovingly enthusiastic service of others.

NOTES

1. Karl Rahner, *Servants of the Lord* (London: Burns and Oates, 1968).

2. Ibid.

3. Keith Clark, *An Experience of Celibacy: A Creative Reflection on Intimacy, Loneliness, Sexuality, and Commitment* (Notre Dame, IN: Ave Maria Press, 1982).

4. Peter G. van Breeman, "Unmarriageable for God's Sake," *Review for Religious* 34 (1975): 839-845.

5. Peter G. van Breeman, *Called by Name* (Starrucca, PA: Dimension Books, 1976).

6. Henri Nouwen, *Clowning in Rome* (New York: Image, 1979).

7. Ibid.

8. Ibid.

9. Sandra Schneiders, *Sisters Today* (December 1969).

10. Ibid.

www.ingramcontent.com/pod-product-compliance
Lightning Source LLC
Chambersburg PA
CBHW070029100426
42740CB00013B/2634